£5

BUSES

YEARBOOK 2015

Edited by STEWART J. BROWN

PUBLISHING

KEY

BUSES
YEARBOOK 2015

FRONT COVER: **One of the models which supported the resurgence of Alexander Dennis was the Enviro200. This example is seen in Dunoon with West Coast Motors.** STEWART J. BROWN

PREVIOUS PAGE: **In the days when most buses had a two-person crew, an Eastern Counties Bristol Lodekka pauses in Bury St Edmunds bus station.** TONY WILSON

BACK COVER (UPPER): **Among the vehicles entrusted to a teenage bus driver by OK Motor Services was this Alexander-bodied Atlantean.** DAVID JENKINS

BACK COVER (LOWER): **Stagecoach operates large numbers of ADL Enviro300s. This MAN-based bus is seen in Dundee.** ALAN MILLAR

Published by Key Publishing Ltd.
www.keypublishing.com

First Published August 2014

ISBN: 978-0-946219-65-0

Printed in England by Berforts Information Press Ltd 23-25 Gunnels Wood Park, Stevenage, Hertfordshire, SG1 2BH

www.busesmag.com

CONTENTS

Alexander Dennis 10 years on

Alan Millar 3

The vanishing

Stewart J Brown 14

The crewed bus

Tony Wilson 20

Not the Grand National

Robert E Jowitt 26

Dart: A short lived service

Billy Nicol 34

A good job – except for one thing...

Gavin Booth 38

Accidentally appropriate

Tim Carter 44

A Tyrolean bus journey

Bob Hind 48

Stagecoach variety

John Young 54

London oddities

Michael H C Baker 60

The final years of Lancashire United

John Robinson 70

I was a teenage bus driver

David Jenkins 74

Cardiff's Ailsas – their last year in front-line service

David Cole 78

Just suppose

Michael Dryhurst & Chris Drew 82

Market day memories

Mark Bailey 92

Stephensons of Easingwold

David Longbottom 98

Battle of Trafalgar

Peter Rowlands 104

Edinburgh demonstrators

Richard Walter 112

A decade of change at Bristol

Geoff Mills 118

LBA Link

Tony Greave 124

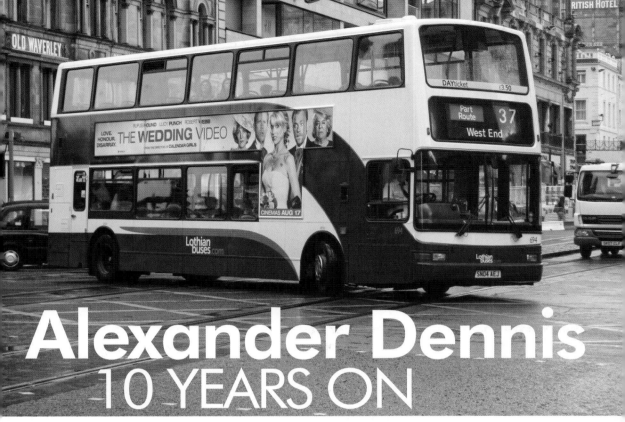

Alexander Dennis
10 YEARS ON

Among the buses caught up in the TransBus collapse and supplied without a manufacturer's warranty were President-bodied Tridents being built at Wigan for Lothian Buses.

Buses editor **Alan Millar** recalls the events that led to the creation of UK's leading bus and coach manufacturer in 2004 and how it has progressed since then.

All photographs by the author

On 31 March 2004, the UK's largest bus and coach manufacturer and the fifth largest in Europe, TransBus International, was placed in administration along with Mayflower, which owned 70% of the business. Ten years on, it thrives by another name, but the outlook then was far from certain.

The troubles stemmed from Mayflower, where accounting irregularities had come to light, prompting the City-listed automotive and engineering group to declare itself insolvent. Within a week of Deloitte & Touche moving in as administrators, 11% of the 2,640 TransBus employees were redundant, many suppliers faced the likelihood of not being paid for materials and

services, while new vehicles were being supplied without the protection of a manufacturer's warranty.

Administrators' prime objective is to realise as much cash as quickly as possible to pay off a stricken company's debts. Sentiment does not figure in their decisions. Hence the redundancies and a determination to sell TransBus and its assets to the highest bidder.

TransBus had only existed since August 2000, when Mayflower and Henlys merged their UK bus and coach businesses into a joint venture run by Mayflower, which had acquired Alexander's bodybuilding plants in Falkirk and Belfast in 1995 and the Guildford-based Dennis chassis business three years later.

Henlys owned Plaxton, which besides being the

3

Stagecoach's business was vital to TransBus and to Alexander Dennis. Among its last TransBus products was this ALX400-bodied Trident in the East Scotland fleet, photographed in St Andrews.

UK's last manufacturer of luxury coach bodies, also had been Dennis's main bodybuilding partner with its Pointer body on the hugely successful Dart single-deck bus chassis, a relationship that was threatened by Mayflower's acquisition of Dennis and its ability to offer a complete product with Alexander's ALX200 body.

Plaxton's main plant was at Scarborough but it also built minibus and midibus bodies at its coach dealership in Anston, near Sheffield and in 1995 acquired Wigan-based Northern Counties, adding double-deckers to its product range.

THREE-BRAND STRATEGY

When TransBus summoned the bus press to Guildford for a presentation of its aims and objectives in January 2001, one of its biggest messages was that the individual brand names — Dennis, Alexander and Plaxton — would be kept, that TransBus was a holding company almost in the background orchestrating manufacturing economies and that those economies would help maintain all five bodybuilding plants.

Within four months, that vision began to unravel with news that the entire Scarborough operation would close, with production of Pointer bodies transferred to Falkirk and slimmed down coach manufacturing moving abroad, possibly to Hungary where Henlys had established a small chassis engineering operation two years earlier to develop an alternative to the Dart.

Labour relations at Plaxton had been difficult for

years and the threat of closure forced the trades union's hand. Just two weeks after TransBus said it would ship Plaxton abroad, a flexible working deal was agreed for the slimmed down coach plant to be located on part of the sprawling Scarborough site. This 'centre of excellence' was headed by one of Alexander's bright young engineers, Brian Davidson, whose leadership skills helped change the fortunes of a business TransBus was prepared to jettison.

Pointer bodies continued to flow out of Falkirk with Plaxton badges at least until early summer 2003, but the three-brand strategy was finished.

As new body-and-chassis products were announced — starting with the Enviro300 single-decker in autumn 2001, the three-axle Enviro500 export double-decker in 2002 and prototype full low-floor single-deck Enviro200 in 2003 — these were badged as TransBus. There was a gradual move — possibly as the old badges ran out — to brand all other buses as TransBus.

The same was supposed to happen with coaches, but the Scarborough plant had a large enough supply of Plaxton-embossed rear number plate frames to ensure that its products retained the name most recognised by coach operators right up to the collapse of TransBus in March 2004.

In September 2003, TransBus revealed plans for a new factory in Falkirk, much larger than the Alexander's site opened in 1958. The official line was that all the other sites would remain open, but this was big enough to absorb the production of all the bus body plants, possibly even the chassis facility at Guildford.

By then, the market for new buses was in one of its downward cycles with production at Wigan reduced to a single line. Loyal customer Stagecoach helped keep Wigan going by accepting 40 Tridents with President bodies in preference to its standard choice of the Falkirk-built ALX400 and subsequently having 24 ALX400s assembled at Wigan.

TransBus also faced increasing competition from the other UK bus body and chassis manufacturers. Wrightbus in particular was gaining ground, having come almost from nowhere in the 1990s to be a significant supplier of large single-deck bodies to major fleets, then repeated this success with double-deckers from 2001.

Optare and East Lancs also were hungry for new business, the former with integral single-deckers and especially the Solo midibus, which challenged the smaller end of TransBus's market for the Pointer Dart, East Lancs with a willingness to offer a wide range of body/chassis combinations, even though it built small volumes.

BUYERS LINE UP

While the TransBus collapse provided opportunities for its competitors, they stood little chance of buying any of the stricken group's facilities, especially as the administrators wanted to sell the business as a single going concern.

The front-runners to buy TransBus included two venture capital companies, London-based Dexter Capital Group and New York-based Cerberus Capital Management, and Chinese consumer goods manufacturer Greencool. Cerberus subsequently acquired several United States bus manufacturers, streamlined their operations and sold them on to new owners.

The big fear in April/May 2004 was that a new owner might not be committed to maintaining the UK manufacturing or design and development capacity.

Against that background, and with the administrators setting an early deadline to complete a deal, two UK buyers — both deeply committed to the bus and coach market — put together packages to rescue almost all the TransBus operations in separate parts, with agreements concluded within six days of each other in mid-May 2004.

First to complete was a four-strong Plaxton management team that acquired the businesses at Scarborough and Anston along with Bus & Coach Glazing, a nationwide coach glass replacement service. Heading the team was Brian Davidson, who latterly had run TransBus's aftersales business. Funding came from Aberdeen Murray Johnstone, a private equity firm that helped finance Stagecoach's expansion in the late 1980s.

There was only one obvious name for the new company — Plaxton Ltd — which adopted Scarborough Castle as its logo and applied Plaxton badging to the fronts of its products to complement the rear number plate frames that survived the previous owner's attempt to extinguish the brand.

The name of the other successor business was just as appropriate: Alexander Dennis Ltd. This was a consortium of Scottish business interests, some of whom already had close links with TransBus and its predecessors.

The Edinburgh-based merchant bank Noble Grossart (another Stagecoach backer) took an initial

TransBus launched the lightweight Enviro300 large single-decker in 2003, with Plaxton front and rear styling on what was otherwise an Alexander structure. This Alexander Dennis example in Worcester was one of 34 new to First Midlands West in 2005.

Before TransBus was formed, Plaxton developed prototypes of its Bus 2000 body on Volvo B6BLE chassis. The front and rear were adopted for the Enviro300, but the project was frozen until the newly independent Plaxton used the structure for its new Centro body. One of the prototypes was acquired by Northumberland operator Henry Cooper Coaches.

40% shareholding. Charlotte Ventures, a private investment company owned by businessman David Murray whose Murray International Metals was a TransBus supplier, took 30%. And Stagecoach founders Brian Souter and Ann Gloag owned the other 30%, Stagecoach having been an important Alexander customer since 1988.

Two former managing directors of Alexander's, Bill Cameron and Jim Hastie, returned respectively as chairman and chief executive, with an urgent need to rebuild customer confidence and restore profits. Cameron had previously headed Hoover's manufacturing business in Scotland and helped run some of Brian Souter's business interests beyond Stagecoach.

Alexander Dennis declined to buy the Belfast body plant and within months concluded that Wigan should also close, effectively killing off the President body developed by Plaxton in 1997. It also closed the small chassis development operation in Hungary, which latterly was an offshoot of the Guildford factory.

PLAXTON RIDES FREE

Freed from past constraints, Plaxton broadened its coach range and returned to the full-size bus market. It dusted down the designs for Bus 2000, a successor to the Pointer body that had been killed off by the TransBus merger, and developed it as the Centro

built eventually on the VDL SB120 and SB200, MAN 12.240 and Volvo B7RLE chassis.

It reopened the mothballed Pointer bus plant in Scarborough, a separate building next to the coach facility with sufficient roof height to build single-deckers but nothing higher.

Plaxton had remained in the small bus market with the Beaver 2 body on Mercedes-Benz Vario light truck chassis, but recognised that the move to low-floor buses would limit its future. It needed a small low-floor bus and turned to former TransBus colleagues to get it.

This was the Primo, developed by Enterprise Bus, a company created by five former TransBus managers to take over the chassis development office in Hungary in July 2004. Enterprise Bus had offices in Lancashire and Budapest and established a factory in Hungary to build buses for a range of global partners, starting with Plaxton.

It was in Hungary because of the collapse of the Soviet Union. Two Hungarian manufacturers, Ikarus and chassis partner Cspel (pronounced 'Cheppel'), provided the lion's share of motorbuses and coaches to Soviet Bloc countries and possessed considerable engineering expertise. Before 1989, Ikarus was the world's biggest volume manufacturer of buses, but business fell away rapidly in the 1990s and Henlys had recruited some of its skilled people to set up the

Hungarian development office in 1999.

Enterprise Bus had a vision of being like a manufacturer of soap powders for supermarkets, producing a standard bus that its partners would badge as their own. It called the bus the Plasma.

It was 7.8m long by 2.4m wide, with a stainless steel integral structure, four-cylinder Cummins ISBe engine, Allison automatic gearbox and a Z-drive layout that gave it a very short rear overhang and proportionately long low-floor area. The deal with Plaxton saw Enterprise supply powered Plasma body shells, which were then glazed and fitted out at Scarborough with up to 28 seats.

While the design was innovative, it proved troublesome in service, with early production examples suffering from unacceptable levels of vibration. Major rebuilding became necessary and only 169 were built for the UK with the last delivered in 2010.

Before itself going out of business, Enterprise also supplied seven left-hand-drive dual-door examples to a Hungarian customer and 15 to New Zealand manufacturer Designline for customers in New Zealand and Australia, the first of these being completed by Plaxton.

Coach developments at Plaxton brought wheelchair accessible versions of the Primo and Panther bodies on Volvo chassis and a 15m Panther on tri-axle Volvo B12B chassis primarily for Stagecoach.

A NEW DOUBLE-DECKER

Alexander Dennis's highest product priority was its new Enviro400 double-decker, which it launched in June 2005.

Development began in TransBus ownership, but accelerated after the May 2004 takeover in recognition of the need to make good the lead that Wrightbus had established with its Gemini body from 2001.

The Enviro400 combined a striking individual look — principally a roll-top front roof dome — with a layout that increased lower saloon seating capacity. It became available initially with an updated version of the Trident chassis that underpinned many of its ALX400 bodies but would also be offered on Volvo's then new B9TL chassis, an option taken up only by Dublin Bus, East Yorkshire and Go-Ahead London.

The Enviro200 followed in July 2006, almost three years and a major engineering rethink after TransBus unveiled the first prototypes. In 2003, TransBus believed — with good reason — that at least for London this should have a low floor the full length of the bus, an offside rear engine, super single rear wheels and a second door at the back rather than the middle. Its studies of human behaviour suggested the layout would encourage passengers to spread themselves out and not congregate around the exit.

Unfortunately, forces within Transport for London disagreed. They argued that the rear doors would

A Plaxton Centro-bodied MAN 12.240 operating with MacEwan's at Jedburgh in the Scottish Borders.

A fully framed and powered Primo structure, as built in Hungary, awaiting glazing and fitting out by Plaxton.

A Plaxton Primo of Reays of Wigton operating a city service in Carlisle.

Plaxton continued to build the Beaver 2 body on Mercedes-Benz Vario chassis, latterly with a nearside rear wheelchair lift to meet the accessibility requirements of the Disability Discrimination Act. This example with Munro's of Jedburgh was photographed in Newcastle.

be damaged in bus garages and they also were strongly opposed to moving the wheelchair ramp from the centre door to the front, as proposed on the Enviro200.

Consequently, the production Enviro200 was an updated Dart chassis with an all-new body. Like the Dart, it had a T-drive layout at the back, with seats on a raised floor over the rear axle and engine. And to assure customers that it possessed all the pedigree of its predecessor, Alexander Dennis called it the Enviro200 Dart until the new name became established.

It completed the bus range in November 2007 with an updated Enviro300 that incorporated some chassis refinements and a longer and wider version of the body on the Enviro200. It also supplied it on heavier duty MAN 18.240 chassis for Stagecoach until 2010 and on 45 Volvo B7RLEs for Ulsterbus in 2009.

MERGER AND EXPANSION

Bigger changes came in quick succession in spring 2007. In mid-April, Colin Robertson succeeded Jim Hastie as chief executive. If his predecessor's brief had been to restore customer confidence and financial viability, Robertson's was to expand the company, pledging to double its size within five years and make it into a more credible international competitor.

Not quite 40, Scots-born Robertson came from a senior post with construction plant manufacturer Terex in the United States. Such was his commitment to Alexander Dennis that he bought a shareholding in the business when he joined. Seven years on, Robertson and his family have increased their financial stake while David Murray has sold his shareholding.

The weekend after Robertson joined Alexander Dennis, Plaxton attracted nearly 10,000 visitors to Scarborough to celebrate the company's centenary, a pleasure it could have been denied had events in 2001 and 2004 taken a different turn. Coaches dating back to 1930 were lined up around the factory site and took part in a cavalcade through the town.

Three weeks later, Alexander Dennis announced it had acquired Plaxton, effectively recreating TransBus. Except that everyone was at pains to insist that this time it would only be the good parts of the old business. Past mistakes had been learnt, not least to retain the Plaxton brand.

Plaxton could not have survived much longer as an independent business, as its venture capital backer wanted to cash in its investment and the company needed to develop new products. Other investors who

A Plaxton Elite i-bodied Volvo B11RT for Stagecoach in a promotional livery commemorating 10 years of megabus.com.

One of the first Plaxton Elite-bodied Volvo B12BTs, for Northern Ireland operator Logan's of Dunloy.

A second generation Enviro300 body on an MAN 18.240 with Stagecoach East Scotland in Dundee.

went on to acquire East Lancs and Optare also were interested in Plaxton, but the deal with Alexander Dennis was the most logical fit and the better long-term bet.

At the time, Alexander Dennis said there was limited overlap between its own and Plaxton's customers. Probably the biggest shared client was Stagecoach, which bought coaches and not buses from Plaxton.

To begin with, there were suggestions that the Centro body would survive alongside the Enviro200 and Enviro300, with customer choice determining which models continued, but maybe that was wishful thinking. Centro production ended in 2010, with the last examples — on Volvo B7RLE chassis — going to

Blackpool Transport and Veolia.

However, this by no means spelt the end for bus production at Scarborough. Quite the opposite. With demand for Alexander Dennis products rising, starting in November 2007 production of substantial numbers of Enviro200s transferred there from Falkirk, reversing what had happened just over six years earlier when TransBus moved Pointer production to Scotland.

Enviro200 production has gone on growing at Scarborough, in the same building that produced the Pointer. An even more radical move was to switch some Enviro400 production to Scarborough — body and chassis assembly — from Falkirk and Guildford, achieved by dividing the coach plant (which has the headroom for double-deckers) in two with aluminium bus body assembly kept separate from stainless steel coaches.

This has included hybrid electric double-deckers, and all the first production new generation Enviro400s were built there from spring 2014.

The previous autumn, when an industrial dispute threatened to disrupt production at Falkirk, Colin Robertson described Scarborough as the company's 'premier' production plant, praising the efficiency and flexibility of its enlarged workforce. Any idea of the TransBus 'super plant' in Falkirk was well and truly dead.

NEW COACH PRODUCTS

Moving bus production into part of the coach plant is a sign of how the traditional part of Plaxton's market has contracted in recent decades. The swing to heavy duty chassis has reduced the need for operators to replace coaches as often as they did over 30 years ago, and traditional activities like day excursions, extended tours, private hires, schools and workers' contracts are in long-term decline.

Today's buyers of new coaches divide even more starkly than before into retail and fleet customers. Retail are the small, family-owned independents buying single figures of coaches every year. Sometimes the ultimate single figure of one.

Fleet buyers are the likes of National Express contractors, Stagecoach, Ulsterbus, Oxford Bus Company, Shearings, Park's of Hamilton and the Ministry of Defence. Other than Shearings and the MoD, these all are heavily involved in meeting growing demand for scheduled express coach travel.

Competition for both sectors' business is fierce and there is little sense of patriotism to be detected. Even state-owned Ulsterbus has bought mainly Irizar-bodied coaches from Spain in recent years, while most NatEx business has gone to Caetano in Portugal and Shearings has favoured Setra from Germany.

Alexander Dennis ownership and the transfer of bus production has helped Plaxton absorb the impact of the changed demand for new coaches, but it has also enabled it to invest in a succession of new products to compete across the many subsectors of the coach market, fleet and retail.

Plaxton was already well advanced with a new version of its Cheetah midicoach on Mercedes-Benz Vario chassis before the takeover and launched it that summer. A Euro 6 replacement is expected in 2015.

The pace of development has been impressive, starting in 2008 with the Elite, reviving an old model name for a new premium model (initially on tri-axle Volvo B12B chassis) targeted at buyers looking for more than was available on the highest specification Plaxton Panther. A two-axle Elite (on B9R chassis) followed in 2009.

A second generation Panther, with elements of Elite styling, came next in 2010, then a Scania chassis option with the Panther in 2011.

In 2012, primarily for Stagecoach which needed higher capacity coaches for its megabus.com express services, it launched the 15m inter-deck Elite i on Volvo's new tri-axle B11R. Most passengers sit above the level of the driver, with a few additional seats and a wheelchair area beside and behind the driver, creating space for over 70 passengers.

This layout means that where the original Elite has a sleek, bulbous front, the Elite i is box-like, the effect tempered by styling touches from the 'proper' Elite. Besides Stagecoach, Cardiff-based New Adventure Travel and Irish operator Matthews have taken the Elite i, while PolskiBus — the Polish express

Plaxton launched its new-look Cheetah midicoach, on Mercedes-Benz Vario chassis, in July 2007.

The third generation Plaxton Panther body, with elements of Elite styling.

An Enviro350H hybrid single-decker of Stagecoach Bluebird in Aberdeen.

coach operator owned by Sir Brian Souter's Souter Investments — has taken the first left-hand-drive examples, creating the possibility for Plaxton to seek more European export business, something it last tried in the early 1990s.

A shortened B9R-based Panther — the Panther Cub — followed in spring 2013, aimed at a market niche that Plaxton and Volvo might otherwise lose to competitors.

In October 2013, a third generation Panther appeared with even more Elite styling and for the other end of the market Plaxton introduced the Leopard, a lower specification coach for the private hire and school transport sectors, based initially on the B9R and its Euro 6 successor, the B8R.

With Leopard, Panther, Panther Cub and Cheetah in its zoo, Plaxton was steadily recycling old Leyland chassis names to go along with its own reuse of Elite from 1968.

The Leopard filled a gap created by the earlier demise of the narrower Profile body on the Volvo B7R and on Alexander Dennis's own Javelin chassis, which was dropped after sales volume fell below a level that would justify keeping it in production.

HYBRIDS AND VIRTUAL ELECTRICS

In the UK bus market, hybrid electric has been the main area in which Alexander Dennis has displayed innovation.

This picked up where TransBus left off, as the old company unveiled a hybrid version of the original full low-floor Enviro200 in 2003. First word of its revived plans came in November 2006 with a partnership with a company part-owned by Rolls-Royce, but that had been set aside by a year later when the first fruits of a new tie-up with BAE Systems were ready to show — hybrid Enviro400s and Enviro200s with BAE's HybriDrive system already proven in North America.

Thanks to Transport for London and Green Bus Fund finance from the Department for Transport in England and the Scottish Government, Alexander Dennis has shared in the sales of hybrid buses made possible by public money offsetting the additional cost over conventional diesels.

As the hybrid electric parts are largely the same on both models and double-deckers are more expensive than single-deckers, the percentage price premium for double-deckers is lower. Consequently, far more Enviro400Hs have been built than Enviro200Hs.

Alexander Dennis also developed a full low-floor 12m hybrid single-decker with up to three doors — the Enviro350H — initially in left-hand-drive for Spain, but also secured orders for 26 single-door models for Stagecoach and First in the UK, with a variation of the Enviro300 body.

Its longer term aim is to develop viable all-electric

ADL launched the new generation Enviro400 in May 2014. This prototype is built to London specification.

buses, with four 'virtual electric' Enviro350H hybrids expected in service in 2015 with First Glasgow, using roadside charging to allow them to operate for much of the day without drawing on the diesel engine.

The company's biggest disappointment in these endeavours was to lose out to Wrightbus in the competition to develop what has become the New Routemaster, the three-door, twin staircase hybrid double-decker for Transport for London, for which its rival has so far won orders for 608.

It has also made two unsuccessful attempts to acquire Optare, whose Solo would fill a gap in the Alexander Dennis model range.

INTERNATIONAL EXPANSION

All the UK bus manufacturers are chasing export business, to increase their production volumes and reduce exposure to the peaks and troughs in home market demand.

Alexander Dennis has picked its fights in arenas where it believes it has the best chance of winning. It has steered clear of much of Western Europe where the big players like Mercedes-Benz, MAN and Iveco

A covered-top Enviro500 operating a sightseeing tour in San Francisco.

sell thousands of mass-produced three-door standee single-deckers and concentrated instead on places either with a tradition of buying high-capacity double-deckers — Hong Kong and Singapore especially — or are open to persuasion that such vehicles can fit in their future plans.

It has done well in parts of the United States and Canada with the Enviro500, both as a commuter bus and as an open-top sightseeing bus, even with

A long wheelbase Enviro400H hybrid for Reading Buses.

some Enviro400s. It has also sold 70 Enviro500s to a Malaysian customer and developed hybrid versions.

The other plank of its export drive has been with the Enviro200, offering a lighter weight vehicle with good passenger accessibility. New Zealand, Australia and North America have all taken this bus.

Many of these buses are assembled locally from kits shipped out from the UK, thus meeting either an expectation or — in the case of the United States — a demand that federal-funded buses are built there. It has established partnerships in the US with ABC Industries to build the Enviro500 and with major manufacturer New Flyer for the Enviro200, while Kiwi Industries builds the Enviro200 in New Zealand.

In Australia it went one stage farther, in June 2012 acquiring leading bodybuilder Custom Coaches, which began assembling UK-designed products along with its established products on other manufacturers' chassis. However, a downturn in business led it to place Custom Coaches in administration in May 2014.

Back home, the main effort has been updating the bus range for the change to Euro 6 diesel engines. Known internally as MMC (for Major Model Change),

this is bringing a new family of buses designed to overcome weaknesses of its predecessors and with far more common parts than before on double-deckers, small and large single-deckers.

First to appear, in May 2014, was the new Enviro400, with an all-new Enviro200 expected six months later.

It has continued to build on other manufacturers' chassis. Driven by policy at Stagecoach, the Enviro400 has been built on Scania N230UD chassis since 2008 for a growing number of customers and the Enviro300 on Scania K230UB single-deck chassis since 2011. It has also bodied the compressed natural gas-fuelled K270UB for Stagecoach and Reading Buses.

A revived relationship with Volvo has begun with 18 Enviro400-bodied B5LH hybrids for Stagecoach in Dundee.

Sales in Alexander Dennis's 10th year in business exceeded £540million from a global workforce of around 2,000 and generated a profit of £20million, much of which has been invested in future product development. A far cry from the precipice on which the fatally wounded TransBus teetered in spring 2004.

The Vanishing

Some were well-known; some almost unknown. **Stewart J Brown** catalogues some of the names to have vanished from the list of bus and coach makers active in the UK in the last 20 years.

All photographs by the author.

The bus and coach manufacturing industry is in constant flux. A struggling manufacturer comes up with a winner – Dennis and the Dart – and becomes a major force in the market. A prestigious international coach maker decides that the small British market is not really worth the expense of developing new right-hand-drive models – Setra – and pulls out.

There is an ebb and flow, as makers come and makers go. Some change names. What follows are some of the major names to have disappeared from the list of bus and coach suppliers in the UK in the last 20 years

ALEXANDER BELFAST
Alexander Belfast was formed in 1969 when the Scottish coachbuilder purchased the Potters business,

to which it had previously subcontracted the assembly of some Y-type bodies. The company was predominantly a supplier to Irish operators, but found itself under growing pressure as Wrights of Ballymena expanded. It was a victim of the TransBus collapse, closing in 2004.

AUTOSAN
You can be forgiven for not having heard of Autosan. The first UK examples of the rather basic Eagle entered service in 2005 – three in Britain, plus one for an Irish operator. In its home market, Poland, it is sold as the Orzel and is described by Autosan as a "functional and comfortable coach adequate for long travels and interurban communication".

By 2010, when the last were delivered, there were around 70 in the British Isles, most of them 70-seat school coaches.

AYATS

Spanish manufacturer Ayats still builds coaches, but is not currently supplying the UK. Its designs have over the years been striking, and its best-selling model in the UK was the 4m double-deck Bravo. The company had sold a few coaches in Britain in the early 1980s, then re-appeared with the Bravo in 1998. One of the most surprising customers for the Bravo was Translink, which took 25 in 2006 for operation on express services in Northern Ireland.

BLUE BIRD

Blue Bird is a US-based school bus maker, and in 1994 it appointed a UK dealer, Alan Wilson of Leicester. Small numbers of Blue Birds were sold to local authorities as school buses, and a few went to small operators as low-cost coaches. First took 20 Blue Birds in 2002 to launch its Yellow School Bus programme, and that was the end of Blue Bird in the UK. Blue Bird was, for a short time from 1999, owned by Henlys, at that time Plaxton's parent company.

BMC

Turkish builder BMC offered a wide range of buses and coaches in the UK. Its main coach was the integral Karisma 35-seater, formerly known as the Probus. The Probus appeared in 2003 and was initially not the most reliable of vehicles, so some minor restyling and a new name for 2007 were intended to close that chapter in BMC's history. There was also the Nifty or the Midilux, a front-engined 27-seater.

BMC's most successful bus was the 11.9m-long low-entry Condor, with large numbers being supplied to Metro, the West Yorkshire PTE, for use as school buses. There was also a Hawk midibus and a basic front-engined school bus, the 1100FE.

BMC was taken over by the Turkish government in 2013 in a dispute over its debts, but before this happened UK sales were already flagging. The company's future is uncertain. The BMC name reflects the company's origin in 1964 as an assembler of vehicles for the British Motor Corporation.

BOVA

The first Bovas for the UK were Europas, in 1981. Then followed the Futura, which went on to enjoy an incredible 31-year production life. When the Futura was launched in 1982 it was competing with the likes of the Leyland Royal Tiger Doyen, the Duple Caribbean and the Plaxton Paramount. Bova became part of VDL in 2003, and the Futura was subsequently badged VDL Bova. When the new Futura was launched in 2010 it

LEFT: **The BMC Falcon was a low-entry urban bus. It was Chester City Transport's choice for a park-and-ride service, with eight entering service in 2004. This is a 2008 view, by which time the Chester City Transport operation had been taken over by First.**

TOP: **Most of the Ayats sold in the UK have been coaches, but in 2005 Arriva took ten Bravo-based open-top double-deck buses for operation in London on The Original Tour. They were built on Volvo B7L chassis and seated 75 passengers – 51 on the open top deck.**

ABOVE: **Blue Bird's products can best be described as utilitarian. First imported 20 rear-engined AARE 60-seaters in 2002. There should be flashing lights above the windscreen but these are not allowed under UK regulations so, perhaps to make a point, there are orange painted discs where the lights should be.**

The first ever double-decker from DAF was the DB250, initially bodied exclusively by Optare. This is a low-floor model, with Low Rider branding, in the fleet of Reading Buses.

The SB120 was DAF Bus's rival to the Dennis Dart SLF, and was launched with Wrightbus Cadet bodywork. Nine entered service with Go North East at the start of 2003. They were 39-seaters.

With a production life spanning 31 years, the Bova Futura has been one of the longest-lived models in coaching history. The age of this example operated by Swiftsure Travel of Burton-on-Trent is disguised by its Northern Ireland registration. It was new to the company in 1998 and is seen in London's Park Lane in 2004.

The Caetano Nimbus was a neat design, built on Dart SLF chassis. First took 53 with 29-seat dual-door bodies for its London fleet in 2003.

was as a VDL product, with the Bova name consigned to history. The very last of the old Futuras – of which 11,218 were built – went to a British operator, London Mini Coaches, in 2014.

DAF BUS

DAF started selling coaches in Britain in 1975, and branched into buses in partnership with Optare in 1989, first with the single-deck Delta and then, from 1992, with the double-deck Spectra. Britain's first modern low-floor double-decker was a redesigned DAF/Optare Spectra, in 1998. The Dutch company's bus and coach manufacturing business was acquired by VDL in 1993, although it wasn't until 2003 that the brand name was changed from DAF Bus to VDL Bus. This distinguishes the VDL bus manufacturing business from DAF Trucks, which is owned by Paccar, and which manufactures the engines used in many VDL products.

DESIGNLINE

Antipodean buses are rare in Britain, but New Zealand manufacturer Designline provided a few. Stagecoach trialled a hybrid Designline Olympus in 2004, which was the first of ten hybrid Olymbuses used on the Tyne & Wear PTE's QuayLink service in Newcastle from 2005 until 2010, when they were withdrawn and replaced by diesels. The Olymbus, built on an MAN chassis, used a diesel-fuelled turbine which fed the batteries which drove the electric motors.

EAST LANCS

East Lancashire Coachbuilders was based in Blackburn and could trace its history back to 1934. It was for many years primarily a supplier to municipal bus operators. It was known for its versatility – the

An East Lancs Spryte, on a Dennis Dart SLF operated by JP Travel, passes Manchester's Victoria Station.

An unusual Hispano-bodied Volvo B7L operated by McGill's of Greenock. It was new in 2003 as a Volvo demonstrator; this is a 2011 view in Glasgow. The body was called the Habit.

bus industry equivalent of bespoke tailoring - and its bodies appeared on a wide range of chassis.

In 1994 the company moved to a new factory and started producing revised models such as the Cityzen and the Pyoneer double-deckers, and the Spryte single-decker on the Dennis Dart SLF chassis. The Flyte used an Alusuisse structure, and this also featured in the company's new low-floor double-deck body, known variously as the Lolyne (on Dennis), Vyking (Volvo) and Lowlander (DAF/VDL).

In 2007 the business was bought by the Darwen Group, then in 2008 Darwen purchased Optare and the Optare and East Lancs businesses were combined under the Optare name. Bus production in Blackburn ended in 2012. The final East Lancs models were the single-deck Esteem and the double-deck Olympus. The Olympus continued in production as a Darwen Group and then an Optare product. There was also an open-top version of the Olympus, the Visionaire.

HISPANO

The most numerous UK Hispanos weren't promoted under the company's name. The model was the Mercedes-Benz O404 Vita, which was sold in the UK by EvoBus as a Mercedes product, with little mention of the body coming from Hispano. Around 70 were sold from 1997 to 2001. Small numbers of Hispano coach bodies were later sold on VDL chassis in the UK and Ireland – so small the chances of actually seeing one are pretty slim.

Volvo tried to offer Hispano bus bodywork in the UK, on the B7L, and built a couple of demonstrators, including an artic. Indian manufacturing conglomerate Tata took a shareholding in Hispano in 2007, and total control in 2010 at which point the company was renamed Tata Hispano. The business closed in 2013, a victim of Spain's economic difficulties.

IKARUS

Back in the days of the Communist bloc in Eastern Europe, Ikarus was the world's biggest bus maker, building 13,000 vehicles a year. That particular world collapsed, along with Communism, and Ikarus gradually disappeared. Its coaches first appeared in Britain in 1987, initially on Volvo B10M chassis. Buses, on the DAF SB220, followed in 1990. Most of the Ikaruses imported to the UK have been on DAF chassis, the result of a tie-up with dealer Hughes DAF, which later became Arriva Bus & Coach. The last UK coaches entered service in 2001; the last buses, low-floor Polaris models, in the following year.

IVECO/IRISBUS

The Iveco EuroRider was launched in the UK in 1995, and was initially only sold with bodywork by Beulas. It was the company's first success in supplying full-sized vehicles in Britain, following the failure of the Turbocity bus, which it had tried to sell in the early 1990s. Plaxton bodies became available in 2001, followed by Marcopolo in 2005 and Hispano in 2007. The last UK EuroRiders entered service in 2012.

The company made a half-hearted attempt to sell city buses in Britain with the French-built Agora Line city bus, exhibited as a chassis at Coach & Bus 99 but not actually appearing as a complete vehicle, in partnership with Optare, until 2003.

The Irisbus name was coined in 1999 following the merger of the bus and coach interests of Iveco and Renault. It also included Ikarus, from 1999 to 2006. The Irisbus name was dropped in 2013, in favour of Iveco Bus.

While Iveco is not currently active in the full-size bus

and coach market in Britain, it does sell minibuses based on the Daily light truck chassis.

MARCOPOLO

Although never a major force in UK coaching, Brazilian coachbuilder Marcopolo is a big business, producing over 20,000 vehicles a year and with interests in Australia, where it owns Volgren, Canada, where it has a stake in New Flyer, and India where it has a joint venture with Tata. The vehicles sold in the UK were produced at a factory in Portugal, which closed in 2009. The company had been selling coaches in the UK since 1995, initially on Dennis Javelin chassis and then on MANs, Ivecos and a handful of VDLs. There were also a few MANs with Marcopolo's Viale bus body.

MARSHALL

Marshall's prime time as a bus builder was the 1960s, when it was a major supplier of single-deck bodies

For many operators Setra represented the highest quality. This S415HD was new to Dodsworths of Boroughbridge in 2003.

This is an SC Coachbuilders Compass – which was little different from the UVG UrbanStar. This Dennis Dart was one of 34 supplied to Limebourne of London in 1999. It is seen with MK Metro in Milton Keynes in 2007.

to the BET group. The company, based in Cambridge, built double-deckers between 1978 and 1984, and in the 1990s was bodying Dennis Darts and smaller numbers of MANs and Volvo B6s. It also produced an integral midibus between 1996 and 1998 – a troublesome model which, generally, had a short operational life. Marshall ceased bus production in 2002, but its Capital body quickly reappeared under the aegis of Egyptian manufacturer MCV which bought the design rights.

NOGE

Noge bodies were first available in the UK in 1998, and were supplied exclusively on MAN underframes. The key model was the Catalan – a clue to where Noge bodies are built – but in 2006 it introduced the striking Titanium, complete with mock radiator grille. Sales were handled by dealer Mentor Coach & Bus, and when Mentor folded in 2008 Noge slowly disappeared from the UK, after selling around 150 coaches. The company closed soon after, a victim of the recession in Spain.

NORTHERN COUNTIES

Northern Counties was a long-established bodybuilder, based in Wigan. It was bought by its biggest customer, the Greater Manchester PTE, in 1983. A downturn in business saw the company in administration in 1991. A management buy-out followed in 1992, and in 1995 the business was bought by Henlys. The Northern Counties name was dropped with production of the last step-entrance Palatine double-decker in 1999, after which point the company's sole product was the Plaxton President. The Plaxton Wigan factory closed in 2005.

OVI

OVI, Omnibus Vehiculos Industriales, was a Spanish builder which supplied its first UK coach, a Versatile on a DAF SB3000 chassis, to Bibby's of Ingleton in 2000. Around half a dozen were sold in the UK, and a few more in Ireland.

SC COACHBUILDERS

Caetano took over the UVG business in Waterlooville in 1998, and continued with the UVG UrbanStar body, renamed the Caetano Compass. It was replaced in 1999 by the considerably more attractive Nimbus, built exclusively on Dennis Dart SLF chassis. Production ended in 2007. Similarly the UVG S320 coach on Dennis Javelin chassis was developed as the Caetano Cutlass, but few were built.

The first bus from New Zealand to run in Britain was this Designline Olymbus. It is seen on trial with Stagecoach in Carlisle in 2004. It would later become part of the QuayLink fleet in Newcastle.

SETRA

Setra sold its first coach in Britain in 1971, a special one-off order for an Essex operator, Kirkby of Rayleigh. But it wasn't until 1982 that Setra became a mainstream supplier of coaches to the UK. The name is a contraction of *selbsttragend*, which translates as self-supporting. The business was bought by Mercedes-Benz in 1995, with the two brands trading under the umbrella of EvoBus. The Setra name is synonymous with quality, and the company enjoyed healthy sales in the British Isles in the late 1990s and the first decade of the 2000s, including substantial orders from Shearings, Britain's biggest coach operator. However with the introduction of Euro 6 emissions standards EvoBus decided that rather than go to the expense of re-engineering Setra's new 500-series models for right-hand-drive for the UK it would instead focus its attention on the Mercedes-Benz Touro. The last UK Setra entered service in the spring of 2014 with another Essex operator, Talisman Coach Lines of Colchester.

SMIT

Haven't heard of them? Who can blame you. Dealer Arriva Bus & Coach announced in 1998 it would be selling 10.6m Smit Stratos-bodied DAFs. They managed one or two. Smit had earlier been active in the UK in 1982-83. Smit had been bought by VDL in 1996. It closed in 1999.

UVG

UVG, which took over the Wadham Stringer business in 1993 – briefly operating it as WS Coachbuilders – developed the UrbanStar body for the Dennis Dart SLF. UVG offered a coach body, the UniStar, on Dennis Javelin chassis, which was reworked in 1997 as the S320. Neither the UniStar or the improved S320 found many buyers. The company also completed Mercedes-Benz O405Ns for Travel West Midlands. UVG went in to administrative receivership at the end of 1997, in part because of a downturn in orders from the Ministry of Defence, and its factory was taken over by Caetano in 1998, as SC Coachbuilders.

WADHAM STRINGER

Wadham Stringer, based in Waterlooville, Hampshire, made a serious effort to tackle the UK bus market with its Vanguard body in 1979. This was offered on a wide range of chassis including the Leyland Tiger and Cub, Bristol LHS, Bedford Y, Ford R, Dennis Lancet, Volvo B58 and Ward Dalesman. The 1990 Portsdown was built on Dennis Dart and was neither attractive nor successful.

Even less successful was the Winchester coach for the Dart and MAN's midibus chassis. The company was bought by the Universal Vehicle Group in 1993 and renamed WS Coachbuilders. It would be renamed UVG in 1995. ∎

The crewed bus

Before the near universal adoption of one-person operation, British buses usually carried a crew of two, as Tony Wilson illustrates.

Now before anyone gets any funny ideas that the author has finally lost it (it is crewed, not crude), the title obviously refers to buses and their crews, be they operated by a crew of one, two, or just maybe three (you will see what is meant by that later).

With the initial excitement of the New Bus for London project now past, maybe it is time to hail the work of those who propel, serve on and ensure the safe operation of the bus along the highways and byways.

Passengers often take the bus driver and conductor for granted, the priority being that as long as their bus turns up to take them to their destination, all is well. Were it not for the drivers, conductors, inspectors, schedulers and mechanics, where would we be? They are all very much an important part of getting people from A to B. A few of them are illustrated doing what comes naturally to them - or not, as the case may be.

During 1967 Cardiff City Transport took delivery of 16 Metro-Cammell-bodied Daimler Fleetlines. Here in the recognisable surroundings of the bus station in September 1977 one pauses as a driver changeover takes place.

A London Country RT-type AEC Regent III arrives in the open space of Hemel Hempstead bus station, with the conductor ready to perform a perfect moving exit from the open platform. No doubt the present day Health & Safety Executive operatives would have a fit, but back in the days of rear-entrance buses it was normal practice. Some readers will recall the Green and Golden Rovers as advertised on the front of the bus. Golden Rovers were valid on Green Line as well as Country buses, whereas Green Rovers were only valid on Country buses.

An Eastern Counties Bristol Lodekka waits in the bus station at Bury St Edmunds in October 1967, while various crew members meet briefly to pass the time of day. Smart uniforms, ticket machines and leather carriers are on show - and how about a trip to London for just 26s 6d, or £1.30p in today's money?

A United Counties Bristol KSW6B with lowbridge ECW body provides the motive power for the first crew photograph. Here on the outskirts of Bedford the conductor chats with the driver. The bus was new in 1953 and served United Counties' passengers for 20 years.

One of the many services terminating at West Croydon Bus Station was London Country route 402 operated by Dunton Green Garage. During the mid 1970s London Country suffered a chronic serviceable bus shortage. To remedy this vehicles were hired in from a number of companies in Southern England. While most were double-deck buses, there were a few ECW-bodied Bristol MW coaches. This was a Western National coach. Dunton Green Garage was home to these vehicles because there were spare conductors available, and the depot had drivers who were trained on manual gearboxes.

The driver of an ECW-bodied Bristol LH from the BL-class of London Buses, takes a breather and looks like he is in deep contemplation at the rather open and less than inviting bus station in Richmond in August 1977. Or perhaps he was wondering whether he would like to take a turn on the vehicle next to his. Not the traditional London double-decker of the time, this former Leeds City Transport Roe-bodied Daimler with a Gardner engine was on loan from Dennis to assess the Voith torque-converter transmission, which incorporated a retarder for Dennis's new Dominator double-decker, then under development. The Daimler was used exclusively on route 27, running between Richmond and Archway and operated by Turnham Green Garage.

ABOVE: **"Please do not stand up,"** was probably the instruction intoned by the conductor of this Southend Corporation Leyland Titan PD3, as it approached the low bridge over the road near the pier. Seafront service 67 in July 1980 was in the hands of a few of these handsome Massey-bodied vehicles, and ran all the way from Leigh through to the Kursaal amusement park.

RIGHT: **Was the driver of this vehicle named Fred?** Possibly, as it was emblazoned on the door of this Berkhof-bodied Scania coach. Delivered new in 1987 to the East Kent Road Car Co, it was later donated by the company to provide transport for people with disabilities through the Winged Fellowship operation. Here a long way from home way down in the depths of Cornwall in May 1997, staff aid a passenger in a wheelchair boarding via a lift on the nearside of the vehicle after a day's visit to the National Trust property at Trelissick.

LEFT: **A healthy load gives the conductor little time to enjoy the panoramic views across the Solent as this most famous of Bristol Ks operated by Southern Vectis makes its way above Alun Bay in June 1993. As well as the trusty conductor, note also the slatted wooden seats on the top deck.**

LEFT: **Towards the end of 1991 London Buses embarked on a £10million programme to refurbish 486 long-wheelbase RML-class Routemasters. Refurbished RML895 was shown off to the press at a launch by Butlers Wharf close to Tower Bridge in 1992. Thus the bus and a crew duly posed and the clippie performed for the cameras.**

ABOVE: **This may look like an image from the past but this scene was captured in September 2008 at Hawes in Wensleydale. Regular seasonal heritage operation occurs in this North Yorkshire town with vintage buses provided by Vintage Omnibus Services of Ripon and Cumbria Classic Coaches based near Kirkby Stephen. Here two crew members from the former compared notes with a conductor from the latter as the time approaches for the afternoon departures from the town. The bus is an ECW-bodied Bristol LS5G which was new to Eastern National in 1962.**

LEFT: **Now for something completely different. This fine example of a vintage steam bus required a crew of three for operation around the streets of Whitby in North Yorkshire during the 2008 summer season. A driver, a conductor and a fireman, the latter to keep the home fires burning so to speak, operated this Sentinel steam bus originally built as a truck in 1931. Here two of the crew, driver and fireman, take time out between runs, one of them obviously in deep communication Doolittle-like with one of the local feathered inhabitants.**

Not the Grand
NATIONAL

Robert E Jowitt marks rather belatedly the 40th anniversary of a famous breed but, despite various interesting encounters, fails to fancy the creature… or is there an element of doubt?

As wine matures and tastes better as it grows older, sometimes perchance your perceptions of an acquaintance not encountered for many a year - and not much liked when last seen, at that! – will, upon a new meeting, be deemed to have changed and improved, and you will say to yourself 'this is not so bad a chap after all!' I have found that this theory can apply equally to buses, and hatred or at least dislike can slowly melt away into affection. But does this always hold true? Let me discuss this.

Such of our readers as appreciate my words and take note of that which I have written before may recall that now and then I display some fascination with the topic of anniversaries. I suppose I formed the habit, almost the obsession, of remembering dates from the day – or more properly the year after the day – when I first fell in love, or likewise the date of the scrapping of the last Leeds trams, both such events, etched ever in my memory, now well over half a century ago. My family and close friends can tell you this is carried to extremes, with the *n*th anniversary of when I first photographed and, ten years later, acquired one of my own buses; or the date of the bus's first registration, not to speak of family birthdays, all splendid excuse for a bus ride and wine and song.

My buses, as is fairly well known, are mid-1930s Paris Renaults with the celebrated open-rear platform. Of their sisters in general, mostly long since dead, I have offered elegies or articles of mourning in various publications of the omnibus press, first of all to mark the actual demise in 1971, and then, if I recall correctly,

the 10th, 20th, 30th and 40th anniversaries of this final slaughter.

Herewith now, however, though the notion may be deemed repetitive, the subject I offer is intended to prove that I am not too partisan in my persuasions, for I propose to indulge in some reminiscences of a bus which, so I am told, rejoiced not so long ago in the 40th anniversary of its first employment. I must here admit that I actually began upon these pages in the true year of the anniversary, but other matters prevailed and precluded their completion until now. The object however, remains the same; the expression of my feelings for a vehicle in which, I must frankly admit, at least initially, I found little charm or allure, not at all a grand bus, namely the Leyland National.

Before tackling this debatable gem, however, I have a few words to add, in a thoroughly classic Jowitt digression, barely of buses but surely apposite to the purpose, on the matter of anniversaries and old acquaintances. A few years ago I attended the 75th anniversary of the founding of my preparatory school, including verily a service in a cathedral with *two* Bishops presiding (so that afterwards as the company passed out of the west door between the two I could not resist saying 'Bishops to right of them, Bishops to left of them!' at which, plainly familiar with the *Light Brigade,* they chuckled merrily.) In my time at this school there was a chap whom we deemed a weed and a wet and possibly positively odd – some of the others doubtless thought likewise of me – but I remained quite indifferent to him until several years later when, at a society ball for young people, he flagrantly usurped the

One of the principal protagonists of this tale, NPD 111L, ex-Stevenage, in a not very happy moment in all-over poppy red Hampshire Bus days in Winchester.

NPD 111L in the same place, but better fettle. The central exit will be noted. The other bus is a true Hampshire specimen.

Modern street lights and turn-of-the-century architectural splendour. The Birmingham Coach Company in Stephenson Street, with a former Greater Glasgow PTE bus.

girl who at that period I totally and utterly adored. I don't know what she saw in him, and, though he faded then out of my life – and she did too - I never forgave him.

A couple of decades later, but prior to this Episcopal celebration, I was engaged in writing an epic novel – not yet published or even quite completed to this day – on the subject of, *inter alia,* the potential of women priests in the Church of England, stage carriage services and their passengers, and hippy buses and the hippy girls who drive them, and, naturally, the course of true love. Now the characters in novels, as is well known, bear no resemblance to any real person alive or dead, so my villain was naturally in this category, and very happily I had him drown in the Rio de Vigo, Spain. It came to me therefore as something of a shock to discover the wretched fellow who had stolen my girl friend proving very alive at the service, and moreover sprouting a great beard and deliberately sitting down in those parts of the ceremony where Holy Writ bade the congregation stand. The rest of the old boys were amiable enough, some even knew I dabbled in buses – 'Ah, it's Jowitt, is it not! The bus king!' – but this was one acquaintance I did not elect to renew. Which brings me back to the burden of my narrative.

Four decades ago I was living in Winchester, when King Alfred was dying. With the death in Paris of my beloved green and cream buses but 18 months before, I now had to face what was plainly soon going to be another decimation of more green and cream buses, the fleet of Chisnell's King Alfred Motor Services. All too rapidly it was all too true, the standard (dare I say stodgily boring?) fleet of Hants & Dorset VRs, REs and the like was taking over. Literature abounds on the longevity or otherwise of King Alfred buses in the hands of Pants & Corset so I will not dwell on it.

Be it remembered that not long before, in January 1969, the newly formed National Bus Company, as a result of the 1968 Transport Act, had swallowed the former Tilling Group companies – including Hants & Dorset, nationalised in 1948, the BET companies being thereafter likewise swallowed. Here again, literature abounds, so no more elucidation on this.

Now so far as I can recall there were no Hants & Dorset Leyland Nationals serving Winchester at the moment of the King Alfred demise, but I must have known of their existence through the pages of *Buses,* probably seen them elsewhere, and they soon turned up, the personification of the future... the National Bus Leyland National in all its reality, foul National poppy red, rather square, fairly ugly, with that curious camel's hump on the rear of the roof and, as it passed you, that fearsome clattering din from the windmill fan enmeshed in the rear rump. I did not like it at all!

Of course it may be argued that I find it on the whole very difficult to like new buses anywhere anyhow, but the situation in Winchester was exacerbated by three of the few modern buses which I really could and did admire, King Alfred's brave venture in Metro Scanias, being stolen, not long after the Hants & Dorset victory, to operate in Stevenage where the National arm of London Country already operated some similar Scanias. The origin of these latter and thus their presence in Stevenage is fairly obscure to me and now – as applied also then – I have little interest in ascertaining final details; the outrage lay in the loss to Winchester of the Scanias and their replacement with three nasty common London Country Leyland Nationals, logistically sensible no doubt from the Stevenage point of view but an insult or a rotten trick for Winchester.

One facet of the exchange which may have appealed on paper (to those who organise such devilments) was that the Stevenage Nationals, like the King Alfred Scanias, were graced with front and central doors. I cannot say I recall King Alfred making much if any use of the middle doors, and Hants & Dorset made probably even less.

What was more noteworthy about the exchange, at least to they whose eyes are caught by such trifles, was that while the registration plates of the King Alfred Scanias ran AOU 108, 109, and 110J – this being in line with traffic manager John Sincock's policy of using registration numbers as fleet numbers and thus establishing the Scanias at the end of a series which had started with Tiger Cub NHO 101 in 1955 (not without intrusions of other number series in the interim) – the invading Stevenage Nationals boasted NPD 108, 110 and 111L. One wonders whether Sincock, who had been transferred from King Alfred to H&D along with the buses, had managed to put a finger in the pie, or influenced someone else. Surely it cannot have been sheer coincidence! And one wonders too why NPD 109L didn't come to Winchester, rather than 111...

I hazard my belief, *en passant,* that these NPDs, built in 1972, were the oldest Nationals to be employed by H&D, which statement, along with the fact that I did not like them or any of their followers, may bring down upon my head tirades of corrections and horrified protest from their devotees.

I must maintain, regardless, that numerical cantrips or conundrums proved scant compensation, not just for loss of Scanias but also for the invasion of poppy

Hampshire Bus in Stagecoach stripes on the left with apparently asinine name – The Forty-Niner – and somewhat vague about destination, and on the right completely virgin and unidentified but clearly on a local route. The location, in the 1980s, is self-explanatory.

A Hampshire Bus National squeezes through a 10ft 9in bridge.

red buses which were the same – and equally boring – everywhere you turned all over the country... save only some were green instead, as bland a green as the poppy was brash; and on some of them the rear camel's hump was shorter, and then, on some later ones, not at all, in fact the later ones were modified to look slightly less stark altogether. And one saving grace, they could go like... well! I shall never forget coming up on a late evening 47 from Southampton to Winchester in perhaps 1983, really flying, though perhaps this was partly attributable to somewhat romantic circumstances attaching to the journey. What I must state here, however, is that Leyland Nationals were not at all the rule on the 47, but very much the exception, and their intrusion onto a time-honoured double-deck route was brought about by the introduction of a new toy or device digging up a collapsing Victorian sewer in Southgate Street, the principle entry and exit for buses from the south into Winchester; this gadget caused the entire road to be blocked for several weeks, and diversions included – with various lengths of temporary one-way traffic which typical selfish plutocratic motorists of the district tended flagrantly to ignore, only to suffer ignominious reverse in face of oncoming National – the passage of the low arch under the derelict Didcot, Newbury & Southampton

Railway. Hence single-decks, and however little I cared for Nationals these diversions were an irresistible entertainment.

By the time of this merry sport, however, we were some dozen years into the National era; I must hark back to earlier days. I do not propose to write a list of all the places where Nationals might be found, for it would appear merely rather like the index of an atlas, but, before harking forward to some of them I tarry a little while longer in Winchester; as King Alfred vehicles were one by one withdrawn, the ex-Stevenage trio were increasingly far from the only Nationals on the streets of the Old Capital, but nevertheless always distinctive by virtue of those middle doors.

There came to be other distinctions. As if the powers-that-be realised its bleak livery depicted too well the monolithic nature of the enterprise, various local attempts – and almost certainly very necessary – were made to entice passengers aboard. At one time or another Winchester could claim Hampshirebus or Wintonline, at one moment a National borrowed from somewhere in Devon, at another moment an anonymous albino, while sundry Nationals sported names which to me seemed irrelevant and even asinine; I mean who are *Barrow Boy Bill* or *The Forty Niner*? Another, though nameless, was rendered fairly dire with a horrid face designed by a local schoolchild. I think in the 1990s I spotted certain names from Arthurian legends, suitable enough as King Arthur's Round Table hangs in the Great Hall of Winchester Castle, but the buses were no longer Nationals; this, however, was on fleeting visits, because in 1989 I had abandoned Winchester for the Welsh Marches whence I could – and did – foray on buses into the West Midlands or some of those places constituent in what I mention above as items from an atlas index.

I must boast that, contrary to the arguably mistaken practice which I have sometimes pursued of deliberately failing to photograph modern buses because they are too hideous and too much the destroyers of those which I have loved whose place they have usurped, I was bold enough or rash enough or (in hindsight) sufficiently foreseeing to photograph the brutes in reasonable numbers. This may of course be an example of the attraction of repulsion, but in practical terms they served well enough *simply as buses*, even if noisy and ugly, for my studies of street scenes, human life, etc, and as there were plenty of them it didn't matter too much if I occasionally muffed a shot.

It must be obvious, furthermore, that by the 1990s the oldest Nationals were not far short of two decades old, and while many, perhaps newer ones, were still with original owners, a fair quantity had passed on to other operators. There is often, for me, a degree of allure in second-hand buses, some romance about emerging attired in new guise; and though of course the ultimate case here is the descent to non-psv use, to the garb of contractor, fairground or hippy, I never met or heard of a National thus sinking. Nevertheless various examples of second-hand Nationals still in use round Birmingham – alongside those still plying fairly gallantly with original keepers such as Midland Red or West Midlands or whatever title the main lump of PTE buses then espoused – achieved a dashing aura of piratical independence. I remember well a fleet – or perhaps just a small tribe – of Nationals inscribed in grandiloquently sporting spirit as The Birmingham Coach Company. It has to be granted that the jaundiced tint of livery hardly lived up to the promise of the name but it was a change from the old poppy red and for this alone perchance the more exciting.

One, just one second-hand National turned up at Primrose Motors of Leominster, Herefordshire. Primrose was at that date, with a keen new manager, undergoing a major face-lift from previous ill-reputed and scruffy doldrums, and this National was turned out magnificently in resplendent primrose (what else?) with new crest or logo enormous on its flanks, and truly revealed how thoroughly decent a National could be capable of being presented when treated with art and care. I was at that time a part-time driver for Primrose, but I never managed a turn on the National before I and my family uprooted ourselves, in 1999, from Herefordshire in favour of the Isle of Wight… whence Southern Vectis's huddle of bland-liveried Nationals had long since gone to glory or elsewhere, though extraordinarily enough I discovered years later (through gricer grapevine) that one of these victims, Southern Vectis number 878 of 1973 and so one of the earliest, registered XDL 802L, had been re-registered and transmogrified into Ludlows of Halesowen NAT 333A.

And herein a tale; or in fact two tales. Before retreating to the Isle of Wight I had on several occasions visited Halesowen though I cannot now be quite sure why, unless only that, firstly, it was on the way to Birmingham, and secondly, that my sons and indeed I myself were rather taken with the apothecary-cum-model-railway-shop (which is of some repute among cognoscenti). I must note, thirdly as it were, that Halesowen is famous as the birthplace of (if you happen to have heard of him) the once-renowned author of the first half of the 20th century, Francis Brett Young. A dedicated local society has now for several

NPD 111L in new livery – Ludlows – and no central exit, in Halesowen in the 1990s.

Red & White Nationals congregate in Newport.

A National trio in Halesowen, with two Ludlows vehicles framing one from The Birmingham Coach Company. The buses were new to Crosville, Southdown and London Country.

decades been devoted to keeping his name before the public and reviving enthusiasm for his novels which, if on occasion verbose and somewhat dated in style, are thoroughly well worth reading; and not least for many dramatic descriptions of the Black Country and the Welsh Marches with not infrequent passages of local trams and omnibuses.

The highly amusing disastrous bus ride out of Malvern on – we assume – a Midland Red, undoubtedly an SOS, in *Mr. Lucton's Freedom* or the final magnificently moving passage on the boarding of a Birmingham electric tram on the last page of *Portrait of Clare* must rank very high among the best pages of English-between-the-wars novels. Francis Brett Young, obviously, died long before Leyland Nationals saw the light of day. Leyland Nationals, however, proved to be thriving in Halesowen in the 1990s. All in white barring a dash or two of red and blue (tentatively but for no obvious good reason mildly French) and dashingly exhorting (suggesting the apiary) Buzz With Us they were of the neighbourhood fleet of Ludlows. I have sometimes felt that the curious association, by no means rare, between busy bees and buses is not necessarily entirely appropriate, but Ludlow's bees seemed busy enough, and immaculately clean besides… and with that livery they would need to be, wouldn't they.

RIGHT: **A 1984 National 2 in the Badgerline fleet leaves Bristol for Nailsea. It had migrated south from Midland Red West.**

BELOW: **Contrast. Jowitt's favourite Parisian buses alongside a Primrose National.**

I observed further that some pains must have been taken with registration plates, as various could be spotted with three identical digits. It could well be the case that the firm had acquired certain registration plates and re-registered some of the vehicles, a game which is perfectly legal, and certainly applied to NAT 333A ex-Southern Vectis as cited above… and then to my amazement and, I must admit, to my pleasure, who should I encounter? I have to say that there was no longer a central entrance, and a very tidy job had been rendered in replacing it (chop-off from a derelict?) or possibly (which would very much spoil the fun) here was just another re-registration, but whatever the story, what did I see before me but NPD 111L, last seen by me a decade before in Winchester, and long before that (never seen by me) a resident in Stevenage.

Very handsome, all in white, did she look, and I felt besides that I was meeting a long-lost friend. But no, nay, never, it was no more than a chance if

entertaining encounter. Even in that moment of crying with recognition 'Hail, fellow, well met!' (or whatever one should say in identifying a long-lost bus, though that which I have just quoted is good enough for me!) I could not find my way really to admire the Leyland National. Maybe a good chap, if ugly and noisy...but no, 20, 30, 40 years on, I still can't, even now!

In conclusion, none the less, firstly while checking the word *cantrip* which I have employed above but which I thought might raise doubts or disbelief in the opinion of my readers it is accredited in the Concise OED (though woefully excluded by other more condensed works) as *Scots, Archaic* (and therefore surely well familiar to former editor of *Classic Bus, Classic Bus Yearbook, Buses Annual* and *Buses Yearbook,* namely Gavin Booth, and the subsequent excellent and present editor of *Buses Yearbook,* namely Stewart Brown, respectively from Edinburgh and Glasgow) and is defined as 'Mischievous or playful act. Trick'.

Second, while researching through my negatives for a few pictures to illustrate these buses which I conceived as boring I unearthed dozens and more than dozens and in truth considerably more than the reasonable number I mentioned earlier. Maybe they were just the only bus available to illustrate the current street scene (or the backdrop to ephemeral fashion of the girl in the street), but perhaps, though well despised, the Leyland National, even unwilling as I might be to admit the case, was some sort of revolting inspiration, in its heyday, in my transport photographic career. A horrid bus, yes, a cantrip, yes, certainly nothing to compare with something like the Routemaster or the Leyland Titan, surely not a grand National, but never lightly to be denied!

At this juncture I should perhaps take up that wretched novel again, and finish it... but I will not alter the Rio de Vigo, and the tale, whatever buses it may boast, will not include Leyland Nationals.

DART
a short-lived
service

Dart Buses ran services in the
Paisley area between 1996 and
2001. **Billy Nicol** looks back.

ABOVE: **Dart began operations in the summer of
1996 with a fleet of Mercedes-Benz L608Ds. This ex-
Ribble vehicle has a Reeve Burgess conversion.**

RIGHT: **As the company expanded full-size buses
were added to the fleet, with the first being
Leyland Nationals. This bus was built as a Leyland
demonstrator in 1980 and is seen in Glasgow in 1997
on the service to Linwood.**

RIGHT: **Coaches played a very small part in the Dart business. This 1982 Leyland Tiger with Plaxton Supreme body came from OK Travel in 1997 and is operating on the express service from Glasgow to Bridge of Weir.**

LEFT: **New Mercedes-Benz minibuses were purchased, including this example with 31-seat Plaxton Beaver 2 body seen at Paisley Cross soon after entering service in 1999.**

RIGHT: **Following the purchase of an MAN from Thamesdown Transport, Dart purchased eight new 11.220s with Marshall bodies. One loads in Linwood in 1999.**

LEFT: **In the summer of 2001 Dart entered into an unusual franchise agreement with Stagecoach to run some routes from Glasgow city centre to south-side suburbs. A Wright-bodied Dart in Stagecoach Glasgow livery is seen at the Pollok Centre bus station. The bus had been new to Go North East in 1992.**

MIDDLE: **One of the more unusual buses in the Dart fleet was this Leyland Tiger with Alexander P-type body. It has been new to Fife Scottish Omnibuses and was acquired in 2000.**

RIGHT: **Dart did buy Darts, both new and secondhand. This is one of three Dennis Dart SLFs with Marshall bodies bought new in 1999 and operating on a Strathclyde PTE contracted service in Glasgow.**

BELOW: **Optare Deltas were never common in Scotland. Dart operated three, purchased from Westlink in London in 1999. The Delta was based on a DAF SB220 chassis.**

BELOW: **Late purchases in the spring of 2001 were three Leyland Lynxes. This one had been new in 1987 to Sheffield & District, a short-lived subsidiary of Caldaire Holdings. Dart Buses closed in October 2001.**

A great crowd mover. This Alexander Midland Leyland Leopard could carry 77 people, after they had negotiated the three-step entrance. This was a 1964 bus, but generally similar vehicles were still being delivered in 1982.

A good job
– EXCEPT FOR ONE THING …

Keeping the customer satisfied? **Gavin Booth** considers the joys of bus travel.

All photographs by the author

Working in the bus industry, it has been said, would be great if it wasn't for the passengers. It has usually been said in jest but there are times when senior industry personnel have said as much, sometimes even in the hallowed portals of the Traffic Commissioner's office.

Passengers of course are what the bus business is all about. No passengers, no need for buses. But as the single essential ingredient, bus passengers have not always been well served by bus companies.

Let's go back to the early days of motorbuses. Passengers had to be pretty agile even to climb aboard an early bus, and negotiating the outside stairs of an early 20th century double-decker called for a degree of dexterity and courage that can only be admired a century later. The high build was inevitable, given the chassis layout of buses of

this period, and the bodies were just a short step removed from the bodies on horse-drawn buses – but the passengers kept coming.

I have – usually slightly reluctantly – ventured out on the very exposed outside stairs of a few preserved motorbuses while they were in motion, where the promise of a grandstand view from the upper deck offset much of my reluctance. For reluctance read fear. But upstairs is surely the place any self-respecting passengers should sit. And in the real world of the 1910s and 1920s once you were there, usually on wooden seats, you were exposed to the

The way things were – upstairs in an Edinburgh Corporation MCW Orion-bodied Leyland PD2: unlined grey-painted panels, vinyl-covered seats. Efficient (lots of seats) but not exactly welcoming. The author travelled to school on buses like this, and lived to tell the tale.

Information readily available at Buchanan Bus Station in Glasgow.

Real-time information in Brighton, with a 5A arriving on time – and advertising its phone app.

vagaries of the British weather. When it rained, you could either retreat to the lower deck and find a space if you were lucky, or pull your inevitable hat down on your head and draw the canvas cover out over your knees.

Now, you might say that this was a long time ago and now everything is different. Well yes – but there was a time within the memory of many *Buses Yearbook* readers when traffic staff were looking for maximum capacity and engineers were looking for something sturdy, reliable and easy to maintain. The poor passengers were rarely given a look in, so they had to travel on buses like Scottish Bus Group's Alexander Y type-bodied Leyland Leopards, with a steep three-step entrance and 53 seats with space, allegedly, for 24 standees. Great crowd-movers, yes, but hardly the easiest buses to use and certainly not the sort of bus that would lure motorists out of their cars.

But it was not just the on-bus experience. You often needed determination to find where the buses ran and survival skills to cope with shelterless bus stops in exposed places. There were bus stations of course, but many of these had been allowed to deteriorate to the point where the crumbling edifice housed some of the less savoury members of society.

These aspects have largely improved, it must be acknowledged, with increased pressure on bus companies and local authorities to provide comprehensive information at bus stops and stations; comprehensive, perhaps, but often incomprehensible – or simply unreadable, because the typefaces are far too small or the timetable cases are positioned at a height that only suits passengers who are six feet or over. You think I'm joking? Have a look around next time you find yourself needing bus information in an unfamiliar area.

Bus companies used to argue that there was no need to provide information on bus stops because it was assumed that everyone had already rushed out to buy the latest edition of the twice-yearly timetable book. In Scotland these often ran to over 400 pages of closely-set type – I know; I used to proof-read them. And of these 400 pages probably only a dozen were actually relevant to most passengers.

Today, computer technology can allow us instant access to where buses are at any given time, and I can check real times at my local bus stop before I leave home so I can time my journey to avoid long waits.

The quest for passenger satisfaction has occupied a substantial part of my working life, whether helping

Cramped conditions at Merry Hill bus station in the West Midlands.

Passengers waiting in the centre of Paisley have a decent shelter and good-quality bus service information.

to drag Scottish Bus Group into the world of marketing, or subsequently working with Bus Users UK. So I see the hundreds of complaints that pass through our hands and have a pretty good picture of what upsets passengers. Some things rarely change, so bus service reliability causes the most problems followed by driver attitude, issues with frequency and the failure of buses to stop or even show up.

As cars pour on to our streets bus drivers find it increasingly difficult to run to time, particularly where local authorities do not provide bus priority measures like bus lanes and even dedicated busways. And bus operators tell bus users that they are constantly frustrated in their efforts to run to time by roadworks (some unplanned and unexpected), processions and diversions – probably not what Paul Simon had in mind when he wrote about 'accidents

> No Standing allowed in upper deck -Thank you
>
> Il est interdit de se tenir debout à l'étage superieur de ce bus
> Stehen im oberdeck verboten - Danke
> Se prohibe estar de pie en el piso superior - Gracias
> Vietato stare in piedi sulla piattaforma superiore - Grazie
> Yläkerrassa seisominen kielletty - Kiitos
> Forbjudet att stå upp I bussen på övre plan

A friendly multi-lingual notice in a Brighton & Hove double-decker. Foreign language students will probably still occupy a double seat each, though.

and incidents' in his song 'You can call me Al'. Passengers waiting at bus stops often have no way of knowing what has happened and why the bus is so late, while the poor driver of the first bus to arrive after the delay will get it in the neck for something that probably wasn't his or her fault. Mind you, drivers are rarely the most communicative of souls and even in these days of the instant communication, iPhones and two-way radio, they frequently plant themselves in the cab during prolonged delays, choosing not to share any information they may have of the 'what's happening?' and 'how long?' variety.

There are drivers who, you suspect, long for a return to the days of half-cab vehicles, where they can concentrate on driving the bus without pesky passengers bothering them by buying or showing tickets and asking questions.

We have all experienced serially grumpy drivers

Passengers know the fare before they board this
Reading Buses vehicle.

An attractive welcoming message on a Lancashire
United double-decker.

who find it difficult to give a simple 'good morning'
or 'thank-you', but that is not the whole story. I have
been involved in judging awards for Britain's best
bus driver and have come across men and women
who greet every passenger enthusiastically, keep
passengers informed, and – metaphorically speaking,
as we're talking about bus drivers – go the extra mile.

Mystery passenger work is also fascinating, with
the extra attraction of getting paid to travel on buses.
It can be quite daunting to land in an unfamiliar town
or city with no previous knowledge of the bus system
– the way I choose to do it – and spend a day or two
sampling as many routes as possible. Arriving at the
railway station you might be surprised how little
bus information can be displayed, even when the
train company and the bus company are essentially
one and the same. Tourist information centres vary
widely and there are still too many that don't display
bus timetables prominently and where an enquiry
at the counter elicits a response along the lines of
'where do you want to go?'. My answer should be
that if I knew that I wouldn't be asking, but that's
the truth. Until I know what the choices are I can't
make an informed decision. And when I ask why the
timetables are not on public display, the response is
often that they only get limited supplies from the bus
company so they want to hold on to them. Oh dear.

So when I finally find my bus stop, with bags of
information in an ideal world, my next dilemma
is – how much is the fare? I would never dream of
queuing up to buy a shirt at Marks & Spencer or
a pint of milk at Sainsbury's without knowing the
price. Yet that is what many bus companies expect
me to do.

Bus companies argue that they can't show every
fare – and that is reasonable – but a few sample
fares so that I know I need to be ready with coins or
notes would be helpful. And where buses operate a
no-change policy and fail to display fares then I find
myself boarding the bus with a heavy handful of
coins in the hope that I have enough.

As a mystery passenger you are required to check
the condition of the bus inside and out, note the
temperature, seat pitch, how welcoming the bus
appears, how good the driving is, check if there are
proper destination displays, if there is information
inside the bus – you can guess the rest. And there are
bus company managers who travel, even drive, their
buses on a regular basis, and others, you suspect,
who only set foot on a bus when the latest delivery is
handed over by the manufacturers, and who endure
a bus ride to the inevitable lunch. And it's often their

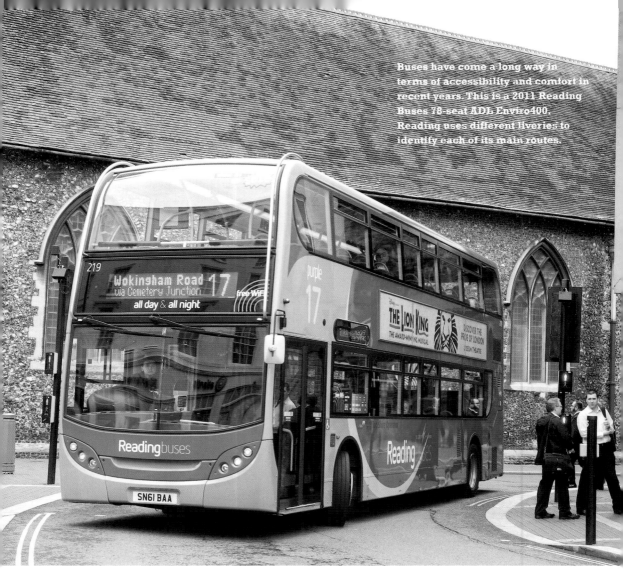

The view forward through 'see-through graphics' from a National Express Dundee double-decker.

buses that are musty, drab and rusting at the seams, with faded, often non-matching and torn moquette and etching on the windows.

And there are still some passenger-unfriendly practices lingering on – like the notices warning passengers about all the things they mustn't do. 'Passengers must not speak to the driver or distract their attention without good cause; must not stand forward of this notice; must not leave luggage in the gangway' – and all of these 'while the vehicle is moving'. Not to mention signs forbidding us to eat or drink or put our feet on the seats; where are the signs welcoming passengers and telling us what we *can* do?

Bus passengers do not deserve this and there is still a wide variation between the best-regarded bus

FirstBus worked hard to improve the interiors of its buses, resulting in what became known as the 'Barbie' interior.

Lothian Buses went down the tartan route for its seat moquettes for a number of years – the starry ceiling was only carried when this bus was new at a bus show.

companies and the rest.

Today, of course, seats are generally more comfortable, and the use of attractive moquettes – or indeed leather – and better-finished interiors and better lighting, make travel by bus a more attractive proposition. And there's always the passing view to enjoy – unless, of course, the windows are covered in what are inaccurately described as 'see-through graphics'. These are the overall adverts that cover all of the windows except the driver's (and I'm sure the advertisers would do that if they could), or indeed the bus company branding that spills over from the metal on to the glass. As a passenger you literally see through a glass darkly, with a sea of dots blurring the outside scene. At night 'see-through graphics' are usually much worse – Heaven help a stranger looking for a particular building or even the place-name on a bus stop or street corner.

Of course bus passengers are not always angels. They do put their feet on the seats and eat smelly food, and dare to stand forward of that notice. And – perhaps less anti-social but still irritating – they mark out their space by putting backpacks or shopping bags on the vacant seat beside them, virtually daring anyone to come and sit beside them, even when buses are busy. They are usually the passengers who claim possession of the gangway rather than the window seat, glaring at other passengers or pretending to be deep in a copy of *Metro*.

Overseas visitors don't always understand the protocol of bus use in the UK, and I have seen European language students spreading themselves throughout much of a bus, each one occupying a double seat. Not really helpful when wheelchair bays and wheelarch intrusion mean that there are certainly fewer seats on offer in modern single-deckers than in that 53-seat Leopard of yore.

Which leads us back to the buses themselves. The move to low-floor vehicles over the past 20 years and the fast-approaching deadline for replacing step-entry buses, means that the Leopard/Y type problem has virtually disappeared and we have buses that are easy to board, cater for wheelchairs and buggies and reflect the current thinking that bus interiors should be warm and welcoming with bright moquettes and facings and even leather seats and free Wi-Fi. They are worlds away from the buses I grew up with, all cold metal and plastics, plain vinyl-covered seating and tungsten lighting. Then, it was all about saving weight and therefore fuel, and this is a theme that the industry has returned to recently.

As buses get more sophisticated and you need more than a screwdriver and a spanner to repair them, so passenger expectations have grown. Bus passengers – paying passengers, even those of us with the concessionary cards – demand and deserve high standards at every point of the journey, from the bus stop, to the information, to the friendly driver, to a comfortable bus that is easy to use and runs to time.

It's not too much to ask – is it?

Accidentally appropriate

Those readers who grew up with the pre-2001 vehicle registration system must occasionally note current-style registrations which echo those used by buses in years gone by. **Tim Carter** has spotted a few.

Prior to the 1974 reorganisation of vehicle licensing offices, many bus companies' vehicles could be easily identified by their registrations. Some operators' vehicles were licensed at offices which had only one series of registration marks. These included Midland Red, whose vehicles carried HA (Smethwick) registration marks, Crosville with FM (Chester), Southern Vectis with DL (Isle of Wight) and Hartlepool with EF (West Hartlepool).

Others used a variety of registration marks, but these were still easily identifiable by those in the know, such as Birmingham with no fewer than 15 of the 23 index marks in the OA to OY series.

The 1974 changes reduced the number of vehicle licensing offices. Some retained familiar letters, but in many fleets new and unfamiliar-looking registrations appeared.

The current system of registrations started on 1 September 2001, with each registration ending in three letters. By chance, sometimes a bus would be issued with a registration where these letters matched the style used in the pre-1974 system. A few examples follow.

VO was one of the registrations issued by Nottinghamshire before 1974. This Veolia Optare Solo in Nottingham's Broadmarsh Bus Station is registered YJ56 WVO.

Under the old system CO was a registration issued by Plymouth and carried by many Plymouth Corporation buses. In 2001 this Plymouth Citybus Dennis Dart SLF was registered WA51 ACO.

OF was one of the marks issued by Birmingham. In 2007 Claribels bought a pair of VDL SB200s with Wrightbus bodies, one of which was YJ57 BOF, an apt-looking registration for a bus serving England's second city.

Leamington Spa was once served by Midland Red buses with HA registrations. Today the main operator is Stagecoach Midlands, whose fleet includes KX56 KHA, an ADL Dart/Pointer.

BC registrations were carried by many Leicester Corporation buses. This unusual Caetano-bodied Dennis Dart SLF, KU02 YBC, is seen in the city running for Thurmaston Bus.

Many of the buses operated by the Bristol Omnibus Co had HY registrations. Most of what were the Bristol company's services are now run by First, whose fleet in the city includes Volvo B7TL WX55 VHY. It has a 74-seat Wrightbus Eclipse Gemini body.

Another Leicester registration mark was JF. This Wrightbus-bodied Volvo B7RLE operating for First in Leicester is KX05 MJF.

Among the registrations once issued by Derbyshire was RA. In 2003 Derbyshire operator Felix added Wrightbus-bodied Scania YN03 WRA to its fleet.

An apt registration, but in a different way, is carried by this First Volvo B9TL which is registered AU58 ECW – the initials of Eastern Coach Works of Lowestoft, the destination of this bus leaving Great Yarmouth on the X1 Excel service from Peterborough.

A Tyrolean bus journey

Bob Hind, who entertains *Buses* readers with travel tales from the UK, dusts off his passport to tackle Alpine bus services in Austria.

All photographs by the author

Running buses in the South Tyrol region of Austria must be like having two very differing jobs on the same patch. From May to October the landscape is lush and colourful as the Alpine flora springs into life but by December the whole area has become submerged in several feet of snow under which it will remain until the summer cycle takes hold again.

Consequently there are two differing markets for the two operators that provide the links along the length of the Otztal Valley from Otztal Bahnhof (Station) in the north, 30 miles south to Obergurgl on the Italian border where the Alps meet the Dolomites and the road runs out, at least in the six winter months.

Otztal Bahnhof stands at the mouth of the Otztal Valley, 35 miles west of Innsbruck on the Innsbruck - Bregenz railway line. Not surprisingly one of the bus operators is owned by the state railway. Osterreichische Bundesbahnen, the OBB-Post Bus, was sold by the Austrian postal service to the Austrian rail service in 2005. The other bus company has more local roots: the Otztaler company was founded by the Scheiber family in 1929 and that name dominates the area through which its main line now runs.

Austrians prefer lines to route numbers (probably more about state funding) so the OBB Postbus route along the valley is 4194 and the journeys operated by Otztaler are line 8352. Fortunately the services are co-ordinated and the identity numbers do not appear on the destination blinds, all of which are digital and give detailed route information. The 'Linie Otztal' runs daily throughout the year, between half-hourly to hourly, and takes about 90 minutes to complete the 51 kilometres, sticking faithfully to the 186 road with only one occasional variation at Langenfeld, halfway up the valley. At any time of the year, it is a journey worth doing as the valley is towered over by dramatic peaks, many over 3,000 metres high, which in the summer reveal the erosion of thousands of years caused by the endless waterfalls, and in the winter are blanketed by glistening snow.

My last trip to the region was in July so I was able to experience a couple of the 'branch lines' off the 'Linie Otztal', one of which is only possible in mid-summer. Obergurgl, at the south end of the valley,

is a growing collection of hotels, primarily for the winter ski market, and some remaining farms that have survived the commercialisation of the last half century. It is a popular skiing resort with almost six months of guaranteed snow each year, standing, as it does, at 1,930m above sea level. Its fame dates back to 1931 when Swiss explorer Auguste Piccard became the first man to fly into the stratosphere and then landed his balloon, by design or accident, in the little hamlet of Obergurgl. His adventures are commemorated by a memorial in the centre of the village square which is also the terminal for the valley's bus lines.

A Postbus 4194 was to take me a short way down the valley at 07.45 (it was five minutes late), where I would connect with an Otztaler bus to take me into the next valley to Vent. Fares are not cheap on these routes; the 15-minute journey to the fairytale-named Zwieselstein costs €3.30, but the fare scale seems to be very coarse as the next fare, €4.20, would take me twice the distance. During the 10-minute wait at Zweiselstein for the connection to Vent, I was reassured by the digital bus stop display which counted down the minutes to the next arrival. Obergurgl, at 1,930 metres above sea level, is the highest parish in Austria. Our descent to Zwieselstein reduced that by 480 metres. At 08.12, two minutes early, the line 8400 appeared and we, me and four others, commenced the climb back up to 1,900 metres at Vent.

This mountain road is kept open throughout the year so a regular daily service between Vent and Solden is also maintained. Half way up we were reminded how essential the road maintenance can be. A quarter mile stretch was being completely rebuilt which meant that traffic light controlled, single file traffic, had to negotiate a rough track and numerous heavy duty vehicles through the re-construction. Fortunately traffic was not heavy and the roadworks only caused a couple of minutes delay so that our arrival at the end of the cul-de-sac was just on time.

Vent nestles in the foothills of the Otztals highest mountain, the Wildspitze (3,774m). It has been the site of a permanent settlement since around 550BC. Like many of these village routes, a quick reversal outside the Hotel Similaun, led to a prompt departure at 08.35 on its return journey to Solden. This time we were joined by a crowd of hikers, complete with tons of equipment, so that the bus was soon fairly well laden. An American lady stopped the bus outside the post office to get some assurance from the driver that the next bus would give her a connection to Innsbruck. Whether it did or not, his limited English seemed to be enough to calm her and we continued downhill towards our second encounter with the roadworks. Somewhat concerningly, the driver was then interrupted by a call on his mobile phone which led to a conversation that lasted the remainder of the journey which was completed single-handedly.

The Vent bus, an Otztaler Solaris, approaching Solden.

Around twisting Alpine roads, this was not for the faint-hearted but my travelling companions seemed completely unfazed.

On the outskirts of Solden, having just passed Otztaler's local depot, I left the Vent driver, still in earnest conversation on his mobile, to wait for my next mountain experience. Even in summer, the Otztal Glacier road at Solden is a spectacular experience. The 13-kilometre road climbs over 1,300 metres to the glaciers at Rettenbach and Tiefenbach; the two are connected by the 1,750-metre Rosi Mittermeier Tunnel, Europe's highest road tunnel. All year skiing and adventurous walkers mean that Otztaler runs line 8404 throughout the year, as frequently as every 15 minutes. Drivers have to share the roadspace with cows and goats at regular intervals, creating an unusual hazard when there is a sizeable drop on one side of the carriageway. The glacier road is tolled so even bus passengers have to pay a premium to use it. The journey is not cheap. The single fare is €7.10 and the toll charge €5.50 so the one-hour round trip will cost you marginally less than €20.

The experience is worth it. The 09.11 journey wound its way skyward with just half a dozen passengers on board. The views down the Otztal valley beyond Solden were soon surpassed by the craggy snow-

In the square at Obergurgl, with the memorial to balloonist Auguste Piccard, Postbus line 4194 prepares for the 570m climb to Timmelsjoch.

covered peaks. In the valley the temperature was in the mid-twenties, we were now in the snow fields and it could have been any time of the year. At Rettenbach we were joined by 35 hikers for the remaining part of the route through the tunnel to Tiefenbach. Ambitious (and experienced) walkers can walk down to Vent from this point but I was more interested in a coffee before I prepared for the long descent, by bus.

At 10.20 I was reunited with the Vent driver (minus his mobile) I had left over an hour earlier. He drove with the confidence of a man who had done this before but thankfully fell short of recklessness so that his passengers were able to appreciate a spectacular panorama as we steadily descended back to the valley. Although the upward timetable at this stage in the morning was every 20 minutes, the downward was only hourly. So, surprisingly, two of every three arrivals made the journey back down the mountain, presumably to depot, empty and out of service.

Solden is the biggest community in the Otztal Valley, its population grossly inflated in the winter by the skiing community. Its resident 3,500 population is swamped by up to 15,000 tourists in mid-winter making it the third most popular resort in Austria after Vienna and Salzburg. Amazingly the tourist ski market has been popular here for over 100 years since the road from Otztal to Solden was opened in 1903. The discovery in 1991 of 'Otzi the Iceman' near the Tisenjoch glacier established that the area had actually been occupied since 3200BC.

Not surprisingly Otztaler carry half the number of passengers in the summer period that they carry

The Postbus Citaros have three doors, as seen on this Timmelsjoch-bound bus.

in the winter, even though there are more summer routes open. My return to Obergurgl at 11.26 on 'Linie Otztal' was this time on an Otztaler 8352, albeit nine minutes late. At the northern terminal of the line, Otztal Bahnhof, connections are made with the main rail line and, less frequently, occasional bus journeys to and from Innsbruck. A number of the journeys continue from the station to Imst, a small industrial and administrative centre, 15 minutes west.

This short Alpine excursion was just a taster for my second journey, planned for the following day, which can only be attempted between June and October and is certainly not for those who have any fear of heights.

In April of each year, snow clearers start to move eight-metre deep snow from the Timmelsjoch High Alpine Road which climbs 12 kilometres from

An impressive three-axle Setra operating Otztaler line 8352 prepares to leave the Obergurgl terminus for Otztal Bahnhof.

Obergurgl to the Austrian/Italian border 2,509 metres above sea level. The route has been called 'the secret door to the south' as originally it was a smugglers route across the mountains and the modern road is relatively underused, compared to the Brenner Pass, as it is only open 07.00 to 20.00 for five months of the year. Whilst the idea of building such a road was first floated in 1897, it was over 60 years later before the road was completed and a further nine years before it was able to meet up with the Italian side to provide the link into the Italian South Tyrol.

Whilst Postbus runs seven round trips between Obergurgl and Timmelsjoch from the end of June to mid-September, as an extension of line 4194, it joins with Otztaler to run an additional four round trips (line 8405) across the border to Moos (Moso) im Passeier, the first Italian town, ten kilometres on the other side. From there, regular connections to Merano are available although a new visitor to this area will never quite believe he has left Austria at all, as the Alpine scenery and fairytale architecture is far more Austrian than Italian, and German is still widely spoken across the region.

I chose the first 8405 journey out of Obergurgl, at 08.05, which would continue to Moos but I intended to walk back from Timmelsjoch which will be another story in itself. Almost immediately the midibus was negotiating the first of 12 hairpin bends as it speedily climbed to Hochgurgl where we met the toll booths. Again, bus passengers are expected to pay their part of the upkeep of this road and €2.20 was added to the €3.30 single fare. The 25-minute climb ended, for me, just short of the border where the old customs buildings still stand, their redundancy caused by the European Community. The descent into the Passeier Valley is even more dramatic with tunnels, more than 40 hairpin bends and sheer drops on many sections of a narrow carriageway, often devoid of safety barriers. Scary enough by car, but by bus?

If mountain climbing is a little too energetic, mountain climbing by bus is the sensible way to view this magnificent landscape. The modern fleets of Otztaler and Postbus are comfortable, reliable and the drivers usually welcoming with a smattering of English. The drivers are obviously allowed entertainment to take their minds off the stresses of Alpine travel as every bus I used had a transistor radio in the driver's cab. However the general standard of driving and reliability was good even if bus travel in Austria is not cheap but the views, and the experience, are definitely well worth the fares.

A short Solaris operating Otztaler line 8405 leaving Obergurgl for its journey into Italy, to Moos.

Stagecoach
variety

Although the current Stagecoach fleet is, in line with almost all fleets of any size through the ages, highly standardised, it is still possible to find unusual vehicles within its ranks. Often these have joined the fleet through a business acquisition or they may have been a trial purchase to assess suitability for future mainstream vehicles. **John Young** illustrates a selection from recent years.

Synonymous with Manchester's Wilmslow Road Magic Bus operations for many years were the 20 Dennis Dragons with Duple Metsec bodies that originated in Kenya, and which also worked on megabus.com routes in the early days. This one is seen in Withington Village heading out of the city.

A Stagecoach Routemaster is perhaps not that unusual in many ways, but RML2671 (also known as 12671 in the company's numbering scheme) is notable on account of still carrying London red livery and operating a Lake District tourist service between Windermere and Bowness in the summer of 2013.

This is one of two Optare Spectras delivered new to Bullock's of Cheadle, where they claimed to be the first low-floor double-deckers in Greater Manchester. They joined the Stagecoach fleet in 2008 when most of the bus side of the Bullock's business was acquired, working from Stockport depot until they moved to Sharston and gained Magic Bus livery in 2014. These remarkable survivors had their ranks swelled at the end of 2013 when Stagecoach purchased the Norfolk Green business.

This East Lancs-bodied Volvo Olympian came to the group with the Road Car business and is seen in Lincoln. It is a long-wheelbase 88-seater and was new in 1996.

The Road Car acquisition in 2005 brought a fascinating selection of vehicles to Stagecoach, including a batch of Volvo Citybuses which had been new to Burnley & Pendle. One heads out of Lincoln to Ermine on a former Lincoln City Transport route.

Yorkshire Traction had an incredibly varied fleet when Stagecoach bought the company in 2005. Seven East Lancs-bodied Scania OmniDekkas were then among the newest buses. They are currently split between Chesterfield and Ecclesfield depots; one works Sheffield cross-city service 88.

Seen at a Wythall Transport Museum event celebrating the 50th anniversary of the Daimler Fleetline, this Roe open-top example was new to Grimsby-Cleethorpes Transport who standardized on the type for a time. Currently based at Chesterfield, it spent the summer of 2014 back home at Cleethorpes helping out on service 17.

Stagecoach only had four buses with Northern Counties Palatine II bodies, all from the same batch bought new by Bullock's. Two of them are seen outside Manchester University on the busy Wilmslow Road corridor plying their trade as Magic Buses. Members of the batch ended up as far apart as Kent and Scotland.

The Wirral operations of First, acquired at the start of 2013, brought with them six Alexander Royale-bodied Olympians, the only examples of the type to be operated by Stagecoach. Only this one received group livery, seen here leaving the former Crosville Rock Ferry depot to undertake an afternoon schools run.

The Rennie's operation is far from typical for Stagecoach or any other large group. Many vehicles carry this attractive livery, and private hire and schools work makes up a large proportion of the business. This Mercedes-Benz Touro illustrates the point at Fort Augustus.

This ex-First Volvo B7TL/Wrightbus Eclipse Gemini was the only one of the type to be repainted prior to moving from Merseyside to Scotland. It is seen on a cross-river service on Borough Road in Birkenhead, less than half a mile from the author's first home.

One of two former Eastern Counties Bristol FLFs retained for special events, the other one being an open-topper, arrives at the 2008 Showbus rally at Duxford. The Lodekka was new in 1966 when Eastern Counties was part of the Tilling Group.

A former First Manchester Volvo B7RLE/Wright Eclipse Urban is seen in Wigan having worked from Bolton via Westhoughton on service 540. Rapsons and Road Car were other providers of this combination, whilst it has also been bought new for Cambridge Busway services.

Two small batches of East Lancs Kinetic-bodied MANs were bought new in 2006 and 2007. This one is seen on the Perth to Aberfeldy service; the other batch was new to West Scotland and carried Strathclyde PTE livery when new.

The Volvo B7TL/Wrightbus Eclipse Gemini combination already existed in the group thanks to Road Car, but the sale by FirstGroup of its Wigan depot and its Wirral operations both provided more. This was one of ten at Wigan that were used on services 32 (from Wigan) and X34 (from Leigh) along the East Lancs Road in to Manchester. Their stay there was but brief and they soon found their way to Fife, working from several depots before congregating at Glenrothes in a fleet standardisation exercise.

There are now almost 100 Optare Versas across the group, with examples acquired from Fleet Buzz of Hampshire and Norfolk Green, 14 dual-door examples in London and others operated for several local authorities, including long-wheelbase Transport for Greater Manchester yellow school buses at Wigan. A significant number were bought new and carry standard livery, as shown by this example in Croyde, North Devon.

Bluebird of Middleton had three early TransBus Enviro300s in its fleet and these remain at the Middleton base, along with a former TransBus demonstrator that was a long-standing member of the Stagecoach Manchester fleet. This one is seen in Moston just weeks after the Bluebird takeover.

It remains to be seen whether this type of bus will be considered unusual in the years to come. One of the first batch of 17 for Sunderland, with another 23 to follow, this is a Scania K270UB gas bus with ADL Enviro300 body.

LONDON ODDITIES

For most of its life London Transport strived for vehicle standardisation. **MICHAEL H. C. BAKER** looks at various non-standard types over the years.

All photographs by the author or from the author's collection except where shown otherwise.

t was perhaps inevitable that an organization as vast and as standardised as London Transport should nevertheless put into service a number of buses which did not conform to its standards.

These fall into three categories. The first consists of purely experimental vehicles which proved to be dead-end cul-de-sacs – if a vehicle can be a cul-de-sac. The second are those which were prototypes which led on to production runs. And the third are vehicles which differed markedly from London standards but filled a niche, the World War 2 austerity Guys, Daimlers and Bristols being obvious examples, or others which were only required in limited numbers and were bought off the shelf and were basically of provincial design. The term provincial has rather fallen out of use today, but it

still has currency in the bus world: one only has to think of the regular cascading of buses from London to elsewhere, ie the provinces.

I'm restricting this survey to the years 1933 to 1970, more or less. The first date marks the creation of London Transport, the second the hiving-off of the Country Area to the National Bus Company. The vast majority of the fleet which the London Passenger Transport Board inherited in 1933 came from the London General Omnibus Company, and the former simply carried on where the latter had left off. Design work was carried out at Chiswick works in West London, which had opened in 1921, and the creation of London Transport made little difference to it. The LGOC types already in production, notably the STL-type AEC Regent double-decker and the T-type AEC Regal single-decker were simply perpetuated, although constantly updated. London Transport worked very closely with AEC - their factory was just up the road at Southall - which supplied most of its vehicles.

Perhaps rather curiously it was in single-deckers, which formed a relatively small proportion of the fleet, that Chiswick and Southall were at their most innovative. LT employed single-deckers, other than for Green Line work, only if there were restrictions

London's 1936 5Q5 single-deckers with front-entrance Park Royal bodies can be seen as the forerunner of more modern types, such as the postwar AEC Regal IV.

The Q-type was an advanced design. London operated five double-deck models, including this Country Area bus with 56-seat Weymann body which had originally been conceived as a Green Line coach and had a centre entrance. The engine location behind the front wheel is clearly visible. It was new in 1934.

London's six-wheel Q had bodywork by Park Royal and is seen here in Green Line livery when new, in 1937.

on the use of double-deckers or on lightly-trafficked routes in the outer suburbs or in the country. One obvious disadvantage of the single-decker was that it had a much smaller capacity than the double-decker, and in an effort to address this AEC had introduced the Q-type in 1932. This had an engine placed on the offside of the chassis in a position which released more space for passenger use. Chiswick built a very handsome, strikingly modern-looking body which could accommodate 38 seated passengers, an increase of eight on what had hitherto been standard. Much impressed, LT went on to order three production batches of Qs for use both as buses and

coaches and had 233 in service by the end of the decade.

LT also put into service five double-deck Qs, four four-wheelers and one six-wheeler, but the seating capacity of the four-wheelers, 56, was no greater than that of the standard STL double-decker, whilst the six-wheeler of 1937 was a 51-seat Green Line vehicle. It is said that trade union objections prevented it ever operating as a coach, and it was not until June 1938 that it entered revenue earning service, at Hertford garage on bus route 310.

All five double-deck Qs were most handsome vehicles but were very much a lost cause as far as LT was concerned, being taken out of service on the outbreak of war in September, 1939 and never running in London again. This was in great contrast to the single-deckers which, despite being of such unorthodox design, were kept hard at work throughout the war and beyond. I remember the Birmingham Railway Carriage and Wagon Company-bodied Country Area ones well, which worked out of Reigate garage until replaced by RF-class AEC Regal IVs in the early 1950s, and the Park Royal-bodied Green Line versions based at Guildford and Hertford garages. The coaches had a full width cab and a dummy radiator, as if LT was not totally committed to the innovations which the engine layout made possible. I have no memory of the 5Q5 version, although I must have seen examples in the Kingston area. This, which also had a Park Royal body, was the true precursor of the RF with its entrance ahead of the front wheels and 37 seats. Although many undertakings bought one or two Q-types, nearly all of them the double-deck version, none adopted it with anything like the enthusiasm of LT.

The double-deck Q buses bore a certain resemblance to STL857 which, following the fad of the 1930s, had a full-width streamlined front. Streamlining when applied to, say Gresley's wonderful A4 class Pacific locomotives of 1935, the same year as the streamlined STL 857, could be a thing of dazzling beauty; but it was distinctly inappropriate for a double-deck bus destined to spend its day trundling through the congested streets of central London. A re-numbering as STF1 made no difference to the fact that drivers objected to its noisy cab and engineers to the difficulty of access, and by the end of 1938 it had reverted to half-cab layout and didn't look all that different from a standard STL.

If STF1 is a forgotten one-off, the next double-deck development resulted in what many consider the

This remarkable concoction was an attempt to modernise London's double-deck buses. AEC Regent STL857 – later renumbered STF1 - was new in 1935. It was rebuilt with a conventional half cab in 1938.

definitive half-cab double-deck bus. I refer, of course, to RT1. Ken Blacker in his history of this iconic vehicle, *RT, The Story of a London Bus,* describes it as "the most remarkable (bus) ever to have graced the streets of London".

The AEC Regent chassis was completed at Southall in June 1938, but as Chiswick was still working on the body, it was fitted with, incongruously, an open-staircase Dodson body of 1932 vintage. One of the features of the RT chassis was its low bonnet line so whilst the Dodson cab was replaced, it still gave the impression that the driver was sitting half way between the lower and upper decks.

After some months of experimental use it went back to Chiswick at the end of 1938 and on 3 April 1939, Frank Pick, London Transport's managing director and the driving force in putting London Transport at the forefront of the world's great urban transport systems, inspected the completed RT1. Various minor changes were made and it then began a round of publicity events.

RT1 is still with us. Now that statement may provoke the Disgusteds of Tunbridge Wells or, indeed Chiswick and Southall, to hold up their hands in horror and declare, "Oh no it isn't." I beg to differ. What we have now is the body of RT1 mounted on a postwar chassis, the original chassis having been broken up in 1946. It seems to me perfectly legitimate to refer to the bus as RT1 because at least 95% of the general public on climbing aboard will declare, "What a handsome vehicle, look at the care gone into the appointments, the elegant colour scheme, the comfortable seats, etc," not "Wow what a wonderful chassis!"

Although setting the standard for the huge RT fleet and all its spin offs, RT1's body has always, as the pioneer, featured subtle variations on those that followed. One curious repeat of history occurred in

Was this the definitive half-cab double-decker. With its stylish four-bay body, RT1 set new standards in bus design. There were detail differences between it and the production vehicles which followed.

early postwar days when a Tilling ST open-staircase body was fitted to a new RT chassis which toured garages about to be allocated RTs.

I'm not sure that the many variations on the RT quite fit our theme of experimental one-offs but I think we may legitimately include the Craven version. Because chassis production was outstripping that of the main suppliers of bodies, Park Royal and Weymann, various other manufacturers were invited to supply bodies and whilst most conformed very closely to the LT standard, the 120 supplied by Craven did not, being basically a slightly modified version of their provincial double-decker. Internally they were certainly easily identifiable as members of the RT family but externally they were of five-window layout, had a more upright front and a more sloping back and were thus a most interesting variation for we bus spotters of the late 1940s. They were dispersed in ones and two all over London and the Home Counties, a number going to the Country Area whilst, in my locality, both Croydon and Elmers End garages each had a couple.

Time for more time travel so we'll beam back to the late autumn of 1937 when a very curious vehicle, to wit TF1c, appeared in the streets of Tunbridge Wells, no doubt frightening those in the spa town of a particularly sensitive nature. This would have been on account of its cab which looked as if it had been intended to form part of a greenhouse but had been at the very last moment transferred to a Green Line coach, but not very securely, giving the impression that it might drop off at any moment.

Having successfully introduced the AEC Q, LT decided to invite Leyland Motors to join the fun of putting the engine in unexpected places. TF1c's engine was under the floor but despite this it was given a half cab which made it rather difficult to see where the advantage lay. Two production versions followed. On both the cab, although still affording the driver excellent visibility, looked as if it had been designed at the same time as the rest of the vehicle and the 12 private hire TFs were very handsome. The 75 TF Green Line coaches served as ambulances during the war but resumed Green Line service afterwards and lasted until swept away by the RFs. One survives in the official London Transport collection.

Then there were the CRs. The Leyland Cub was London Transport's standard, normal-control, one-man operated, 20-seat single-decker, but the CR, whilst still seating only 20, was a very different

In 1939 12 TF-class Leyland Tiger FECs with underfloor engines were delivered for the private hire fleet, with 33-seat Park Royal bodies incorporating a radio (the aerial is on the roof) and glazed cove panels. All but one were destroyed in a bombing raid in 1940. LBPT

beast, having its engine at the back. Once again, and really quite ludicrously, it had a half cab. CR1 appeared in January 1938, went into service and resulted in an order for 48 production vehicles. CR1 had a much neater cab than that on TF1 but its short body had a step half way along it, which was not perpetuated in the rest of the type. The last did not arrive until war had broken out and they proved rather troublesome. As this was no time for Chiswick to get involved in fiddling about with a 20-seat temperamental prima donna the CRs were banished into storage. They re-appeared after the war but were never much loved although two, plus a chassis, have survived into preservation.

During the war LT had thrust upon it Daimlers, Guys and Bristols with some very third-rate bodies, but it also managed to lay hands on some Leyland TD7 Titans, again with austerity bodies. Sadly the TD7, finished off under wartime conditions, was nothing like as good as the much-appreciated 100 TD4s in service, and was heartily disliked by drivers.

With the huge demand for public transport generated by the cessation of private motoring because of the war LT decided that it would run double-deckers on some hitherto single-deck routes, but because they passed under low bridges Chiswick was given permission to build some lowbridge bodies which it would fit on to existing STL chassis. There were 20 and they looked pure Chiswick, a very neat adaption of the standard late STL body

During World War 2 the government allowed some chassis manufacturers to construct chassis using pre-war components, the so-called "unfrozen"chassis. This 1942 STL-class Regent is one such bus, with a Chiswick-built body. The registration is in the same FXT-series as the considerably more modern RTs which had been delivered in 1939-40.

The "Meccano Set" was the nickname given to STL2477, a 1938 Regent which was rebodied in 1950. It is seen at Alperton garage. G. A. Rixon

to lowbridge layout. However internally they were very basic, very much to austerity specifications. They had a single front indicator and none at all at the back. These were joined by some highbridge austerity STLs. Another wartime STL variation was the 34 unfrozen chassis which AEC was allowed to complete. These were basically of provincial Regent specification. They were fitted with a variety of bodies. LT also acquired ten lowbridge austerity Daimlers.

Quite the oddest of the STL one-offs was the "Meccano Set". This was STL2477 which in 1950, whilst large numbers of the class were going for scrap, was fitted with a brand new body, developed by Chiswick engineer Arthur Sainsbury. He had the idea for a body made of prefabricated parts which were bolted together, hence its nickname, and was encouraged by LT to develop it and eventually construction took place and was completed in May 1950. In appearance it was clearly a member of the STL family, although all window corners were rounded and, surprisingly, it was painted in the attractive red and white livery which had been obsolete for some years. It ceased passenger work at the end of 1953, then found employment as a staff bus and a trainer. Mysteriously it is recorded in February 1955, by which time there were very few STLs still on LT's books, as being used "on saloon heating and humidity tests on Central and Country routes 6 and 406 respectively". It could surely not have actually carried passengers and Colin Reed, a volunteer at Transport for London's archive department who discovered this information, speculates it followed a service bus. It had the distinction of being the last STL in LT ownership, being sold to Harpers of West Hartelpool around September, 1956. Its revolutionary method of construction, which apparently led to a fair amount of rattling, something in my experience elderly standard STLs were prone to anyhow, does not seem to have led anywhere.

The wartime Bristols, Daimlers and Guys are really outside our brief but the Guy Arab chassis impressed a lot of operators who ordered more examples post-war. LT dipped its little toe in this pool, putting into service in 1950 a standard provincial Guy Arab III with Park Royal-designed Guy body, G436. Hopes that yet another variation on the RT theme was about to enter service never materialised and G436 remained a lonely orphan.

In the early post-war years London Transport had to find buses wherever it could, thus more or less standard provincial AEC Regents and Leyland PD1 Titans joined the fleet.

The T type Regal class dated back to 1929 but two final variations were added postwar, 14T12s with standard Weymann bodies and 15T13s bodied by Mann Egerton. This was a body builder new to LT although it had refurbished many double-deck bodies. The Mann Egerton bodies were said to be the company's own design but I've always thought that either there was a great deal of Chiswick input

Early postwar single-deckers included batches of AEC Regals and Leyland Tigers. This is a 1946 Weymann-bodied Tiger.

RTC1 was a striking 1949 rebuild of a 1940 Regent, RT97, which was used briefly as a Green Line coach.

or Mann Egerton did a very good imitation of what LT would have specified. There were also broadly similar Leyland Tiger PS1s, again with bodies by Weymann and Mann Egerton.

We've looked at the wartime lowbridge STLs. Come the 1950s and LT possessed, considering there were so relatively few of them, a very mixed bag of lowbridge buses, some being the last remnants of the once huge ST fleet, of early 1930s vintage. Logically, given that despite wartime difficulties Chiswick had managed to design a lowbridge STL, a lowbridge RT might have been expected. Indeed plans were in hand when the opportunity came to buy 20 standard provincial AEC Regent IIIs with Weymann bodies, a lowbridge version of that fitted to 20 STLs of 1945. There were similarities with the RT chassis although the low bonnet line which was such a distinctive feature of the RT was not one of them. One wonders why AEC did not adopt this for all its Regents, but they didn't. These 20 new buses were painted green and created the RLH class. Another 56 followed in 1952, in both red and green, and would be the very last lowbridge buses in the LT fleet, a few lingering on until replaced by AEC Swifts which, although single-deckers, had a greater capacity than the RLHs. They were, however, infinitely less reliable.

Much of our story would seem to revolve around double-deckers for Green Line work which, although endowed with all sorts of innovative features, were less than totally successful or, to put it another way, complete failures. Enter the RTC. AEC Regent RT97 was damaged in a flying bomb raid in July 1944 and was rebuilt as an experimental pay-as-you-enter vehicle. The experiment was unsuccessful and it eventually returned to Chiswick. It re-emerged in

January 1949 in strikingly different form as Green Line coach RTC1. The front end arrangement was dramatically different, the radiator being banished to the back under the stairs which enabled the front to sport a horizontal grille with recessed headlights and a rounded bonnet rather reminiscent of the TF. It was a most handsome and thoroughly up-to-date vehicle which, whisper it softly, rather made the standard RT look somewhat old-fashioned. We schoolboys were all agog to catch a glimpse of this latest marvel and as it was tried out on a number of routes it eventually appeared on one of the five which served Croydon, passing the entrance to our school in North End where we stood and gazed at it admiringly. Sadly and inevitably its complex heating and ventilating system failed repeatedly. Also, it rolled in a most uncomfortable manner and there was insufficient luggage space. By the end of 1949 it has suffered the predictable fate of downgrading to a bus. It was sold in 1955 but was not a complete failure for various features and lessons learned led on to the Routemaster coaches which were as close to a successful double-deck coach design as Green Line ever managed.

Although there would be far fewer Routemasters than there were members of the RT family – which is not to say 2,760 is negligible – LT decided to build four prototypes compared to one RT prototype, plus one pre-production bus which spent most of its career as a testbed. The Routemaster was a compromise in a way which was not the case with the RT, for when the RT was being planned the private car was still something of a luxury, the double-deck bus was likely to rule the streets of London for the foreseeable future, it would seat

ABOVE: **The biggest fleet of non-standard Routemasters were the 65 forward-entrance coaches built for British European Airways. This mid 1970s view shows a mixture of BEA and British Airways liveries. British Airways was created in 1974 and merged BEA with BOAC, the British Overseas Airways Corporation.**

BELOW: **A more successful prototype for Green Line operation was this Routemaster, CRL4. It had a Leyland engine and an ECW body.**

around 56, have its engine at the front, its entrance at the rear, have a working life of perhaps ten years and be replaced by something not drastically different.

By the time RM1 was presented to the public in 1954 bus travel was in decline – a number of brand new RTs were put in to store that year, not being needed – and car travel was eating into the market both for travel to work and for pleasure. Fuel economy was of prime importance so weight had to be kept down whilst as many passengers as possible needed to be accommodated.

Longer and wider than the RT, RM1 seated 64 passengers but weighed slightly less than the RT. Instead of a chassis it had two subframes. Chiswick designers had been skilful in avoiding a bus which, unlike the MCW Orion much favoured at that time in the provinces, looked internally as if comfort had not been sacrificed, although the colours in the author's opinion were somewhat garish and generally it was not up to the incomparable RT, but then nothing was. There was something slightly old-fashioned about the Routemaster, and the revolutionary rear-engined Leyland Atlantean was about to render the half-cab, rear-entrance double-decker out of date. Who was to

know that the Routemaster would prove not only to be virtually indestructible but would serve London well into the 21st century?

RM1 originally had a minimal route indicator, a weight-saving measure which would soon be abandoned, and whilst the front end design was quite the most revolutionary aspect of its appearance, it needed several tweakings before the production examples got it just right. The next prototype, RM2, looked virtually identical although they were a number of differences, notably improved steering. It was painted green and worked for a short time out of Reigate garage. RML3 – you've spotted the L – had a Leyland engine and Weymann body. Again it looked much like its predecessors. Much more interesting than either Routemasters 2 or 3 was CRL4 which was a coach. LT still hadn't given up on the notion of Green Line double-deckers. It should be noted that the Green Line routes from Aldgate to the east to Brentwood, Upminster and Tilbury had employed standard STLs, followed, after the war, by austerity Daimlers and, from 1950 by some nicely decorated but otherwise totally standard RT buses.

The CRL had a Leyland engine, and an ECW body

and whilst there were slight echoes of RTC1 it had the rather more successful prototype RM front end. It seated 57, later reduced to 55, and actually weighed less than the standard Green Line single-decker, the 39-seat RF. No Green Line vehicle was ever a proper coach as say Southdown or Ribble understood the definition, but CRL4 was definitely rather more luxurious internally than the RT or Routemaster bus versions with slightly deeper cushioned seats and luggage racks. It took up Green line work on the 721 out of Aldgate alongside RTs, then moved to the 711 Reigate to High Wycombe. There seemed to be no greater propensity for travel sickness on the upper deck than the lower and although the drivers found the steering heavy, various modifications were made, seating reverted to 57, it was deemed successful, was reclassified RMC4 and was still working as a Green Line coach when its production brethren began to arrive.

All four prototype Routemasters have been preserved but the story of RMC 4 is much the most remarkable. RMC4 bucked the trend of all other one-off Green Line double-deckers in that it was able to serve a full life as a coach right until double-deck coach operation finished, then became a bus in NBC green livery and when retired from Hatfield garage in May 1979 had outlived all the production examples there.

Earlier we noted that there were 2,760 LT Routemasters. However just as LT had operated a fleet of AEC Regal IV coaches for British European Airways, so it was decided that the greater capacity of the Routemaster would make it an ideal airline vehicle. One front entrance Routemaster, RMF1254, had been built but had never run in passenger service in London, although I did to my considerable surprise get to travel on it on the Shiel Road Circular when on loan – the Routemaster not me – to Liverpool in October 1962. RMF1254 became the prototype for 65 BEA Routemasters, which had to be kept to the original, short 27ft 6in length, so that they could tow trailers.

By this date the 72 seat Routemaster was in service in London, the first 30ft-long examples, RML880-903, having been delivered to Finchley depot to replace the 609 trolleybuses on 8 November, 1961. No great trauma having been caused to other motorists, any more than when the 8ft-wide version of the RT, the all-Leyland RTW, was introduced in 1949, they were deemed a success, and would become the norm from RML2261 onwards.

We have noted that even back in 1956 the Routemaster was in some respects old-fashioned, notably in that the future lay at the back, if you get my meaning. Eleven years later LT finally got round to building its very own Routemaster with an engine at the back, having in 1965 taken the plunge with the purchase of

some Leyland Atlanteans and Daimler Fleetlines with totally provincial specification Park Royal bodies, of a standard far below what Londoners had come to expect.

At this period LT seemed to almost totally lose its way, forgetting how it had once taken pride in providing the very best in urban transport. The Daimlers were considered less unsuccessful than the Leylands and vast numbers were ordered. They had really rather nice LT-designed bodies but mechanically they were a headache and withdrawal began whilst the last of the RTs were still providing yeoman service.

The last AECs bought new for London Transport, the single-deck Merlins and Swifts, introduced from 1966, were even worse. When one considers the family of wonderful AECs, starting with the pre-First World War B type, which had served London so well, this last venture from Southall was nothing short of a tragedy, both for London Transport and AEC, the latter shortly to go out of business.

The one patch of light in this darkness was, or rather might have been, FRM1, the rear-engined Routemaster. By the time of its entry into service the powers that be had decided that for various reasons a bus designed totally in every respect for service in London was no longer a viable proposition. FRM1's body contained 60% standard Routemaster parts

The unique rear-engined Routemaster, FRM1, in service at Roundshaw.

Prototypes of the New Bus for London entered service with Arriva in 2012. The first of 600 production models followed in the summer of 2013.

and it entered service proving, in the words of Ken Blacker in his book *Routemaster* "outstanding in terms of performance and handling". But all to no avail despite even gracing the streets of my home town when it appeared on the local 233 serving the dismal Roundshaw estate built on what had once been London's first airport. Later it took up work on the distinctly more prestigious Round London Sightseeing Tour but was eventually retired to become a museum exhibit of what might have been. To quote Ken Blacker again: "It remains the subject of tantalizing conjecture over what might have been if only things had been different."

Well, many decades later things did become different. In the summer of 2008 London's newly-elected mayor, the charismatic Boris Johnson, announced a competition to design a new London bus. This provoked equal amounts of surprise, disbelief and ridicule, but also a great deal of enthusiasm within the bus building and design industries.

In 2011 a prototype, as yet without engine and only partially fitted out internally, was revealed to the public and I was allowed a look at it at Acton Museum. There were echoes of the Routemaster and even the open-staircase LT of 1929, yet it was totally of the second decade of the 21st century, with a vast number of innovative features, diesel-electric propulsion and an open rear platform. There were actually three entrances and exits. The rear open platform, where the conductor would stand, had a transparent sliding door which could be shut at quiet times of the day.

After much consultation very little modification was needed, and the first New Bus for London, or the LT as it was officially known, entered passenger service on 27 February, 2012, and shortly afterwards Wrightbus got orders to build another 600. Truly miracles do happen.

The final years of
LANCASHIRE UNITED

On 1 January 1976, the Greater Manchester PTE exercised its option to purchase Britain's largest independent operator, Lancashire United Transport, which then operated as a PTE subsidiary until 31 March 1981. **John Robinson** illustrates a selection of LUT vehicles.

LUT was a major customer of Northern Counties for its bodywork, having first purchased from the Wigan-based company in 1941 with a body on a Leyland Titan TD7, followed in 1942-44 by utility Guy Arabs. It was therefore surprising when Metro-Cammell was selected to body ten Arab IVs in 1960-61 (40-49) although the Birmingham builder had also bodied 14 Leyland Titan PD3s in 1958 which replaced the last South Lancashire Transport trolleybuses, this company being associated with LUT. 44 (535 RTB) has just left its terminus in Great Moor Street, Bolton, on 24 August 1976 operating service 542 to Walkden, passing a Park Royal-bodied PTE standard Leyland Atlantean. LUT had become a subsidiary of GMPTE on 1 January that year, but even before then, in 1974, some of its services had been renumbered into GMT's 500 and 600 series, this previously having been service 42. Although by then 15 years old, its immaculate condition demonstrates the pride taken by LUT in the presentation of its fleet. Withdrawal of this batch took place between 1975 and 1978.

Whilst Northern Counties built most of LUT's double-deck bodywork from 1957, standardisation was less evident with single-deck bodywork which was, from the same year, built (in descending order of quantity) by Plaxton, Northern Counties, Alexander, Duple, Marshall and Burlingham. Scarborough-based Plaxton took by far the largest share with 185 bodies; Northern Counties with just 28 was the second-largest supplier. From 1963 to 1974 Plaxton's conservative-looking Highway body was purchased in both bus and coach variants on chassis as diverse as AEC Reliance, Leyland Leopard, Bristol RE and Seddon RU, a total of 112 bodies. Typifying the early Highway bodies with a multitude of short windows is Leyland Leopard 157 (DTF 587B), one of three 36ft-long PSU3s with 50-seat bus bodywork new in 1964, seen departing Greengate in Salford on 10 September 1976 with a short-working of service 38 to Westhoughton. All three were withdrawn the following year, 157 passing to South Wales operator Rees & Williams, Tycroes, near Ammanford.

LEFT: LUT was a strong supporter of the Guy Arab, purchasing over 360 starting with Arab I utilities in 1942, and gradually working through all the marks until the last Arab Vs entered service in 1967. If there was a bus which typified the fleet throughout the 1960s and 1970s it had to be the Northern Counties-bodied Guy Arab 30-footers which came in both rear-entrance and forward-entrance variants, the latter with their characteristic sliding door. The change occurred in 1963 when the final vehicle of a batch of 17 Arab Vs was ordered with a forward entrance; all subsequent Arabs were to this configuration. Representative of these is 286 (ETJ 922F), from the final batch (265-290) which were all withdrawn in 1980, depicted at Wigan bus station on 18 July 1973 operating service 38 to Manchester although, technically, its Greengate terminus was in Salford. LUT's livery had been red and cream, changing to red and grey in 1969, and by the time this photograph was taken buses in the former livery were uncommon. Behind, a Seddon RU with Plaxton Highway bodywork operates service 54 to Leigh via Bickershaw. The general manager from 1956 to 1964 was Charles Oakham, who came from Manchester City Transport and introduced the Manchester-style destination layout seen here which continued until the demise of LUT in March 1981.

LEFT: **Included within the 185 bodies built by Plaxton were 38 Panorama, Panorama Elite and Supreme coach bodies which were purchased between 1965 and 1980. The first of these were Panorama-bodied Leyland Leopards new in 1965 and 1966, totalling 12 vehicles. These introduced a red and grey livery, colours which were later also adopted for the company's buses. 217 (UTC 769D), the final vehicle of the second batch of four, is seen in Liverpool city centre on 30 June 1973. These were all withdrawn in 1979 although 214 was retained as a training vehicle with GMT, receiving fleet livery of orange and white.**

RIGHT: **LUT was an early buyer of the Daimler Fleetline, purchasing its first batch of six in 1962; another 21 were in service by 1965, although it continued to buy Guy Arabs as well. 176 (ETD 946B) was one of a batch of ten delivered in 1964 and was 17 years old when pictured arriving at its terminus in Bewsey Street, Warrington, on 15 January 1981 on service 551 from Leigh via Newton-le-Willows, although displaying the route's former number, 51. This bus was one of only two from this batch which passed into the GMT fleet and was re-numbered 2310. It was withdrawn in 1982. The railway line in the background is the former Cheshire Lines Committee route from Liverpool to Manchester. The location of this photograph has now changed beyond recognition with a new elevated road called Midland Way running parallel to the railway and Warrington Bus Interchange, opened in August 2006, at street level adjacent to it.**

LEFT: **Following on from the 30 Leyland Leopards, an order was placed for 15 Leyland Nationals which were delivered during 1977 in all-over red with no grey relief. 467 (NEN 954R), by now wearing GMT livery in the style applied to LUT Nationals, stands in Spinning Jenny Street bus station, Leigh, on 5 November 1980 waiting to depart with an early evening service 582 to Bolton. Formerly the 82, this was one of SLT's main trolleybus routes until final closure of the system, and dissolution of the company on 31 August 1958.**

Looking slightly the worse for wear, Tommy Goodwin's yard, part of the massive complex of scrapyards in Boulder Bridge Lane, Carlton, Barnsley, is the setting for this view of 74 (514 VTB) taken on 23 July 1975 before its complete dismemberment. One of a batch of 20 rear-entrance Guy Arab IVs with Northern Counties bodywork new in 1961, withdrawals took place between 1974 and 1978, with five, including this one, going in the first year. Three Bristol LD Lodekkas are also in view, awaiting a similar fate. At this time there were no fewer than 15 different breakers here all working on plots adjacent to one another, the greatest concentration of bus scrapyards in the country.

The last new vehicles delivered to LUT, prior to its final absorption into the GMT fleet in April 1981, were a trio of Volvo B58s with Plaxton Supreme IV bodywork seating 55 which arrived in 1980. They were delivered in the distinctive livery of GMT's coaching arm, Charterplan, which for LUT vehicles had red and yellow stripes. 49 (DEN 245W) is parked under the arches at Greengate, Salford, terminus of several LUT and GMT services, on the evening of 13 March 1984, whilst engaged in private hire work. These three vehicles had a very short life, being withdrawn the following year, and were the only Volvo coaches in the GMT fleet until 1985 when it purchased its first B10M.

Whilst deliveries of new double-deckers comprised Fleetlines with Northern Counties bodywork to the PTE's standard design, 20 ex-London Transport Daimler Fleetlines were purchased in 1980 to accelerate the withdrawal of Guy Arabs and allow further conversion to one-man operation. They were acquired from Essex dealer Ensign, which had been contracted to dispose of these vehicles. LT had withdrawn them prematurely due to their perceived unsuitability for operation in London.

I was a teenage BUS DRIVER

David Jenkins looks back 30 years to the joys of getting a PSV driving licence.

I t is perhaps the pinnacle of many an enthusiast's dreams to obtain a PSV driving licence (or PCV, as it has now become). And with the Public Passenger Vehicles Act of 1981 lowering the minimum age from 21 to 18, I had an opportunity to do so while still at university.

But who to learn with – and who to drive for? Oddly, the second was easier, in that a 20-year-old friend had already spent a summer season driving for well-known County Durham independent, OK Motor Services. I too had spent the summer after my 18th birthday with OK, fulfilling various roles including tours administration (collecting the tickets from the agents), surveying the use of PTE passes on the Newcastle service, as a garage hand, and the job I was originally employed to do exclusively, conductor.

In the meantime, it was a case of finding a driving school willing to teach an under-21-year-old. By chance, I picked up a copy of the newspaper launching Midland Fox, which included an article on their driver training services. A call from a telephone box – no other way to communicate from university accommodation in those days – soon saw me travelling from Birmingham to Leicester for an initial assessment.

Midland Fox's normal training bus was 9010, a Leyland Titan PD2A/30 registered HBF 679D. Smartly turned out in the new yellow-fronted livery, it had been new to Harper Brothers of Heath Hayes, and acquired with the company by Midland Red in 1974. Like many buses of its age, it had vacuum brakes, which were not ideal for a novice in the

With proprietor Wade Emmerson at the wheel, OK's OVX 143D makes one of its two regular morning peak trips on the Bishop Auckland town service. Brackets for removable L plates can be seen below the driver's windscreen.

Possibly the 1984 winner of the award for 'Most Modern Training Bus Livery', I've stopped Midland Fox 9010 in the middle of a driving lesson somewhere in suburban Leicester to take its photograph.

heavy traffic often to be found in Leicester.

In all honesty, after more than a quarter of a century, I can't remember much about the experience of driving it, other than that not being familiar with Leicester, I frequently ended up in the wrong place on multi-lane approaches to the city's road junctions, and the instructor had to rapidly re-plan his route to

It was in a GBB-K Atlantean like this, with a nearside staircase, that I nearly came to grief at a roundabout in Newton Aycliffe. Unusually, this one is on local bus work, at the terminus in Newfield; they were mainly confined to schools work on weekdays, and club outings at weekends.

match the lane I had chosen.

As a back-up, Midland Fox had also obtained a Bristol FLF, not a popular choice with the dyed-in-the-wool Midland Red types. After all, they had been use to refinements like power steering and semi-automatic gearboxes on D9s; the crash box Lodekka was a definite step backwards. Still attired in the blue training livery of its previous owners, Bristol Omnibus Co, I asked for a lesson on the beast, which was duly granted. It would be three years before I drove one again.

I also wrote to OK, letting them know that I should have a PSV licence by the summer of 1984. They generously offered to pay for my test if I took it with them, and as a penniless university student (well, not quite – Midland Fox's fees were paid out of my student grant!) this was an offer not to be missed.

To speed up the process, OK completed the application forms on my behalf but, alas, the North Eastern Traffic Commissioner would not accept them without my signature, so a delay obtained whilst the paperwork made its way from Bishop Auckland to Birmingham and back. Eventually, a date was set for my test – now to be in Darlington – and, somewhat later than planned, I made my way up to County Durham. (The delay had the advantage of being able to squeeze in a holiday on the Isle of Man, but that's another story...).

Usually, OK used OVX 143D as a training bus. Another PD2A/30, it was new to Colchester and its regular haunt was twice round the town service on a schoolday morning, driven by OK's proprietor, Wade Emmerson. But it was out of action, and instead, one of the Southdown Queen Marys, BUF 279C, became my training bus.

Two advantages to this were that the full-front made it easier for the instructor and driver to communicate, plus it had air brakes, meaning that stopping could be achieved without what seemed like the several minutes advanced warning needed with vacuum brakes. Additionally, Darlington's streets were generally a lot quieter than those of Leicester. Indeed, my recollection of the actual test is that we stuck mostly to the suburbs, and neither do I recall doing a hill start.

However, there was one place where I nearly came a cropper. Reversing the bus around a corner, I could see that the rear wheels were going to end up on the pavement. Now, in a chance conversation with another OK driver, he had described how his wife had ended up in a similar predicament on her car test. The answer was to stop, pull forward, and reverse again; she passed. Oh well, I thought, nothing to lose; I followed the same procedure and also passed! My instructor wisely took over to drive the bus back to Bishop Auckland.

Still, I couldn't start driving yet: I had to wait for my driver's badge to come through. In the meantime, I was taken out on a Leyland Atlantean, partly to get used to a bus with a front overhang, and partly to master a semi-automatic gearbox. Away from OK's normal routes, I believe we pulled down a telephone wire in one housing estate; no doubt United would have got the blame for that! Finally, my badge arrived – AA57776 – and at the age of just under 19½, I was a fully fledged bus driver, with an all-types PSV licence.

Fortunately, the first day I took to the road was a Sunday, in one of the two former London Transport Bristol LHs. To suit LT, these unusually had semi-automatic gearboxes, but nevertheless my concentration on the driving led me to miss a passenger on my very first journey; I only found out when I picked the woman up an hour later. The rest of the day passed without incident.

It wasn't long before the schools returned after the summer break, and I found myself at the wheel of an Atlantean on a school contract one morning. Now, bearing in mind that drivers learn only on empty buses, it is rather different behind the wheel of an 85-seat double-deck with a full load. As I braked

Although it became my training bus, the usual role for BUF 279C was on a school duty, driven by a mechanic. Climbing Newton Cap Bank into Bishop Auckland, the main road now avoids the steep gradient, by a diversion over the then-disused railway viaduct in the right background.

The 11.05 town service was covered by a one-man duty on a Leyland Leopard, while driver, conductor and Leyland Atlantean went for a half-hour break. One of the worst buses for this duty was UPT 50K, its Pneumocyclic gearbox seeming less responsive than the electric change fitted to most of the rest of the fleet. There was a puff of air from the pedestal every time a gear change was made.

The Bishop Auckland town service ran every half hour, with a journey time of 27 minutes. This was only achievable with a conductor, usually (as in this picture) a regular turn for Lily Etherington. Only two of the OVK-M Atlanteans had power steering, fitted specifically for this duty. I didn't know this – departing the bus station in one of the others, I nearly hit the post office on the opposite side of the road, because the bus needed a lot more effort than I had allowed to make the 90 degree left turn.

approaching a roundabout in Newton Aycliffe, the bus didn't pull up where I was used to it stopping; fortunately, the driver of the oncoming car spotted my predicament, as I gracefully rolled out in front of him. Lesson learned!

It wasn't the only incident for this teenage bus driver. The buses I had trained on had been 30 feet long or less. Many of OK's Atlanteans were 33-footers, and it took little time to adapt to the 36-foot Leopards that made up much of the fleet. However, allocated LGR 566P, the first of a trio of consecutively registered Plaxton-bodied examples, it was only rounding a familiar corner adorned with railings that I found out that unlike its compatriots, this was a 40-foot version: the railings had come perilously close to the bodywork. A little more care was taken during the rest of the shift.

On another day, my conductor complained about my rough driving, and proceeded to give me a lecture on the use of semi-automatic gearboxes. Apparently, he had done the same to my friend on a previous occasion, and we both later learnt that he held no driving licence at all. Rosy memories suggest it was him rather than us, for OK's other clippies and conductors would not have been long in giving an opinion of their driver's performance.

Another happy memory was being asked in Bishop Auckland bus station if I drove buses – the questioner was of the opinion that I didn't look old enough. One limitation of being under 21 was that basically I could only do stage carriage work, since the 1981 Act did not permit young drivers to undertake long distance or private hire work. A plus really, as it meant no messing around with tachographs and European driving hours, plus certainty that work would only be between about 06.00 and 23.00. Also, as I was working in a location away from home, it meant that my knowledge of the area beyond the company's routes was a little sketchy. However, one morning I had to cover a works contract to an unfamiliar town; it must have been a happy company, for the employees directed me cheerfully to their destination.

Alas, it was all too soon before I had to return to university, which included a year working for Western Scottish in the run up to deregulation. I only took to the wheel a couple of times there: once from Ayr to Girvan and back, and an afternoon with a fully-automatic Leyland Leopard on Dumfries town services. However, I returned to OK for the whole of the summer of 1986, but by then I was 21, and no longer a teenage bus driver.

In June 2001, with the Millennium Stadium just visible above the Western Mail building, 403 is in Wood Street en route for The Bay. Its appearance is typical of the refurbished Northern Counties vehicles with brighter livery and electronic destination displays.

Cardiff's Ailsas – their last year in front-line service

A pictorial reminiscence by David Cole.

Cardiff Bus was a late convert to the Volvo Ailsa, taking its first examples in 1982. These 18 vehicles with Northern Counties bodywork were followed by another 18 similar examples over the course of the next two years. In parallel with the Ailsas, Cardiff Bus was buying Leyland Olympians with East Lancs bodywork and would go on to buy a batch of Alexander-bodied Scanias in 1990. Previous to the Ailsas and Olympians, Cardiff's double-deck choice had been the Bristol VRT in succession to the Daimler Fleetline.

By the millennium, Cardiff Bus was anticipating a single-deck based future and investing heavily in the MPD and SPD versions of the Dennis Dart. The

Scanias and the Olympians, other than a trio retained for driver training, had been disposed of but the Ailsa fleet had grown. Added to the original 36 were 12 former Merseybus examples dating from 1982 and 1984 and acquired in 1996, and eight 1984 vehicles from Fife Scottish, which entered service between 1997 and 1999. At the time the final Fife Scottish example entered service, it was expected to be the last double-decker to join the Cardiff Bus fleet. In the event, it held this position for only eight years before a batch of new East Lancashire Olympus-bodied Scanias arrived.

Post millennium, the Ailsa fleet did not remain intact for long with the first examples withdrawn during 2000. These made the short journey to Edwards

Coaches at Llantwit Fadre for use as school buses and many more would follow as the decade progressed, some still giving good service in 2014. Over the winter of 2000-2001, Ailsas continued to be the mainstay of key routes such as the 57/8 to Pentwyn/Pontprennau and the 47/8 to Llanrumney. The fleet probably reached its most diverse in terms of appearance at this time with vehicles at various stages of refurbishment or upgrading and some carrying fairly vivid all over advertisements, even featuring contravision. The former Merseybus vehicles provided the main base for the all-over advertisements and another three of them carried a blue livery dedicated to a contract for UWIC, the University of Wales Institute Cardiff, although even these were occasionally pressed into all-day service.

The end of the Ailsas in all-day front-line service came rapidly during 2001 with service revisions and the delivery of a batch of Dennis Dart SPDs. Those retained for peak-hour and contract use remained a familiar sight, the numbers gradually declining until the last two were taken out of service in December 2007. They survived long enough, however, to ensure that the Cardiff Bus fleet never became all single-deck.

In original condition, Northern Counties-bodied 422 from the second batch heads down High Street into St Mary's Street on a grey day early in January 2001. Several Ailsas received full rear advertising for varying periods, this one appears particularly apt given the vehicle's engine position.

My work took me to the Cardiff area in autumn 2000 so I had the opportunity to capture the majority of the Ailsa fleet on film during their last year or so in front-line service. The following selection provides an overview of the variety to be seen during that period.

Northern Counties-bodied 412 was one of the first Ailsas to be withdrawn by Cardiff Bus. Like many others, it became a school bus with Edwards Coaches at Llantwit Fadre, operating over a decade for them. In June 2002 it was one of many back in Cardiff city centre operating the shuttle service for a Welsh League of Youth (Urdd Gobaith) event.

Former Merseybus Alexander-bodied 438 has been equipped with electronic destination displays in its original apertures but retains its sliding cab door. 438 was one of the few Merseybus vehicles to carry fleet livery, in this case with the long-lived 'pick an orange' bulls eye. In February 2001 it is seen entering the bus station on service 47 for Llanrumney.

425 was one of the Y-registered Northern Counties batch to be refurbished with electronic destination displays and the brighter livery. In March 2001 it is seen loading in the bus station for Llanrumney. Un-refurbished 426 is next in line.

On 16 August 2000, Northern Counties-bodied 424 passes the Cardiff Hilton Hotel inbound from Pontprennau. In the mainly orange livery, it looked little changed from when it had entered service 17 years previously.

Perhaps the most vivid of the all-over advertisements was that for estate agents Peter Alan on Alexander-bodied 439 showing a typical Cardiff suburban property. On a grey day in November 2000, when being pursued past Cardiff Castle by Northern Counties-bodied 425, it still had most of its contravision panels intact. During the next few months, the need to replace damaged window glass changed its appearance, particularly on the nearside.

Rush hour after the end of Ailsas on all-day front-line services could still produce scenes such as this at the exit of Cardiff bus station. In June 2001, the detail differences between the Alexander bodies on ex-Fife Scottish 451 on the right and ex-Merseybus 442 on the left can be compared, most obviously the destination displays and the location of the windscreen wipers.

Alexander-bodied 444 was one of three former Merseybus vehicles to carry the blue livery for the Cardiff Bus contract with UWIC. In April 2001 it was in normal service on one of the last routes to be predominantly operated by Ailsas, the 47. Heading for Llanrumney, it is turning from High Street into Castle Street.

The Alexander-bodied Ailsas from Fife Scottish were the last double-deck additions to the Cardiff Bus fleet for around ten years. All were finished in the brighter livery and fitted with electronic destination displays. 450 is seen outside the Cardiff Hilton Hotel on 16 August 2000. These Mark III Ailsas were among the last to be delivered to the Scottish Bus Group.

Just suppose

Michael Dryhurst and **Chris Drew** consider what could have been planned for London Transport's Country Area buses almost 50 years ago. Fact... or fantasy...

ast-approaching is the 50th anniversary of that momentous decision taken back in 1967 that is enshrined in the Transport Act of 1968, which overturned some 30-plus years of bus operations in London and the Home Counties, and we all know how that turned-out, right? But...that was never the original plan. There was another, which preceded it.

Oh, yes...

Just suppose.

PROLOGUE

Rather in the manner that before the kill a cat plays with a mouse, the fork toyed with the crumpled and flaking fish-finger, on to which she ladled more marrowfat processed peas. But her thoughts weren't on haute cuisine. They were on the immediate past.

She had humbled the arch-patrician John Spencer Wills, head of the multi-tentacled BET empire. Her lips puckered into a self-congratulatory smile as she thought to herself 'Mao could not have done it better!

And all on me tod, none of the toadies.' The smile broadened as she recalled her 'offer'.

'Mr Wills, it is very simple. Either you sell to the Transport Holding Company the bus interests of BET, or...'

Wills remained stoically calm. 'Or...Minister?'

'We, I, simply nationalize them.'

Chuckling, Wills had risen from his desk. 'Ma'am, you're forgetting the BET group has a huge number of institutionalized investors, holding a vast number of shares.'

'Mr Wills, through the inherited railways holdings in BAT/BET bus companies, the THC can virtually match those holdings one-for-one.' Her voice took-on a steely edge. 'And we...I, hold some 49% of that preference stock, your BET bus stock.'

Sitting down, his smile faded rapidly. Repeatedly, he tapped his desk, never taking his eyes off her. 'Current Market Price?'

'Subject to due diligence.'

Having filled her glass with Kristal, she raised it in

Stevenage

Luton

Hatfield

St.Albans

Hemel Hempstead

Amersham

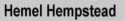

Enfield

Slough

Uxbridge

Romford

Grays

Hounslow

Windsor

Kingston

Gravesend

Croydon

Sevenoaks

Woking

Reigate

Guildford

East Grinstead

Crawley

Horsham

self-congratulation. 'Game, set and...match!'

Eschewing the Kristal champagne for a pint mug of Vimto, she congratulated herself further for manipulating the transfer of London Transport operations to the Labour-controlled Greater London Council, limiting LT to the boundaries of the GLC. As far as she was concerned, the rest was *un piece du gateau*. Simply hive-off those segments of what was the LT Country Area closest to the so-called provincial operating companies, many of which were now THC subsidiaries anyway, and the rest would follow very soon. All to be finalized at tomorrow's meeting.

FIRST ENCOUNTER

With in tow a phalanx of Ministry mandarins, Secretary Sir Berkeley Busby swept into the room, and bowed. 'Minister, thank you for sparing of your precious time-'

'Sir Burkeley.'

'Eh, Berkeley.'

'I thought you went to Oxford?'

'I did.'

'But Berkeley's in California?'

Before he could answer, she turned and studied the large map unfurled on one wall. She pointed to the illustrations of vehicles surrounding the diagram. 'These are... what?'

Clicking his fingers, Sir Berkeley summoned a minion.

'Eh, Minister, the pictures represent...'

The steely gaze froze the minion. 'Eh...eh...'

Sir Berkeley came to the rescue. 'Eh, buses, Minister.'

Squinting, she looked closer. 'Ah...yes! I remember! Used to ride on them to Bradford Grammar School for Girls.' She turned to the Secretary. 'Sir Burkeley...'

'Berkeley.'

'They look very antiquated, very

old-fashioned.'

'Perhaps, Minister...' Sir Berkeley smiled his most unctuous smile. 'Perhaps. But you'll save the day, with your brilliant Bus Grant idea, which will put paid to these dinosaurs.'

'Now, Sir Burkeley...'

'Berkeley.'

'You never informed me you were in banking?'

Flustered, his voice rose. 'I'm not. It's all in the pronunciation.'

'Of course...thus I expect you and your team to sign, seal and deliver this matter, asap. Understood?'

'Incontrovertibly, your Majesty - *Minister*!' He gestured to a door. 'The involved are in the ante-room and...'

She swept out, to be confronted by a number of men. Sir Berkeley rushed forward. 'These are the gentlemen with whom we, I, shall be negotiating.'

As were called their names, each bowed and shook hands with the Minister. 'Eh, Mr Arthur J White, Maidstone & District; Mr Gerald Duckworth, Southdown; Mr Scully, Aldershot & District; Mr Thomas Pruett, Thames Valley; Mr R M Baschy, Luton Corporation Transport; Mr J F Wood, United Counties and last but not least, Mr R F Bushrod of Eastern National.'

Sir Berkeley addressed the Minister. 'Ma'am, these gents have elected as their spokesman, Mr White.'

The Minister studied the Maidstone & District general manager. 'Tell me, Mr White, are you a film-goer?'

White frowned. 'Eh, yes Minister, occasionally.'

Smiling, she surveyed the group. 'Then you're... Chris!'

'I'm usually known as Chalky.'

With an outswept hand, the Minister indicated the group. 'Seven? You're my magnificent seven. Chris was their leader.'

She studied the bemused men. 'Adios!' And was gone.

The meeting took their seats. Noting the size of the group, a minion tugged on a sleeve of Sir Berkeley. The Secretary raised his eyebrows. 'Gentlemen, The Magnificent Seven appear to have morphed into The Dirty Dozen.'

White indicated the representatives of City of Oxford Motor Services, Golden Miller, Safeguard and Tillingbourne Valley.

'Mr White, fine. So now we're...eleven?'

'Mr Secretary, we feel it is relevant for these gents to be present.'

Nodding, Sir Berkeley leaned forward. 'And he...who is he?'

White gestured to an immaculately-dressed and impeccably-presented young man. 'Mr Roger Davies, one of the stars of our Senior Management Training Course. With your permission, we feel he might learn something from all of this?'

Sir Berkeley looked skywards. 'Hopefully...all of us will.'

On the wall was draped still the map, to which Sir Berkeley referred on occasions.

'Gentlemen, with the forthcoming transfer of London Transport to the remit of the GLC, it is proposed that there will be seconded to your companies those relevant areas of the former LT Country Area. Questions will be taken afterwards, no interruptions now.'

He eyed them as would a teacher of miscreant schoolboys. 'Understood? Fine. Right, the Country Area garages will be reassigned as follows. To Maidstone & District will be transferred Chelsham, Dunton Green, Dartford, Northfleet and Swanley. Whatever vehicles are stabled in those garages at zero-zero-one hours on 1 January 1970 will pass to the M&D.'

The general managers were making notes, rapidly.

Sir Berkeley eyed Gerald Duckworth. 'Southdown will assume garages at Crawley, East Grinstead, Godstone and Reigate, while to Aldershot & District will pass Dorking, Guildford, Leatherhead and Addlestone.' In a more than theatrical manner, Sir Berkeley sipped from a crystal tumbler.

Arthur White nudged Duckworth. 'Ten-to-one that's not water.'

'Gin.' Leaning forward, Duckworth stage whispered. 'The gentry always drink gin.'

Refreshed suitably, Sir Berkeley continued. 'Now, Thames Valley. This company will take over High Wycombe, Staines and Windsor, while the bulk of the transfers will be assigned to United Counties, being those premises at Garston, Hatfield, Hertford, Hemel Hempstead, Tring, Amersham, St Albans and Stevenage. The remaining garages will be assumed by Eastern National, namely Grays, Harlow and Romford. And gentlemen, remember that applies without exception, *without* exception, the caveat

concerning vehicles.'

Sir Berkeley checked his pocket-watch. 'Eh, tomorrow. Tomorrow I'll take questions...'

J F Wood stood.

'Sir! I. Said. Tomorrow!'

'Mr Secretary, with great respect, you omitted one...'

'Impossible!'

'Luton?'

Sir Berkeley checked his notes. 'Luton? well, to Luton Corporation Transport, of course!'

'Mr Secretary...'

'Tomorrow!'

Followed by the Ministry minions, the Secretary swept out of the room, which fell silent as the assembled company completed the reading, and writing, of their notes.

Tom Pruett looked around at his fellow GMs. 'Any thoughts?'

Senior Management Course Trainee Davies raised an arm. 'How about I find the nearest pub?'

Amidst cries of 'Cheers!' Gerald Duckworth murmured to Arthur White. 'That boy's going to go far.'

The ever-enterprising and willing-to-please Davies had found a nearby hostelry and with the proffering of a five-pound note, had managed to secure the snug. After all had ingested and digested a generous supping of the events of the day, Arthur White arose.

'Gentlemen, I suggest a couple of proposals. One, we dispatch Roger here to telegraph Secretary Sir Berkeley Busby immediately, to inform him that we are not sufficiently prepared for a meeting tomorrow, hence we cancel that.' This was greeted by a roar of

cheers. Arthur White pressed into the hand of Trainee Davies a crisp ten-shilling note. 'Duncannon Street Post Office. You know how to word it? And don't forget the receipt.'

Davies grinned. 'Trust me.' And exited camera left, rapido.

Arthur White continued his address. 'Now, two. Before our next encounter with Sir Berkeley, amongst ourselves we will convene a meeting to determine our strategy.' Again, cheers and much hand-clapping.

'Okay, given how fragmented we all are, how about a convenient yet convivial venue, relatively easy for all to access?' Applause.

'How about the Ace of Spades? It's on the A3 Kingston by-pass. Together with Gerry Duckworth, an agenda will be set, a 16.00 meet followed by a 19.00 eat. Do I have a seconder?' Once again, the room erupted into rapturous applause.

SECOND ENCOUNTER

The meeting became known as The A3 Royal Flush. At which gathering it was decided that the next confrontation with the men from the Ministry would be held at a site well-away from the cocoon of the Ministry's offices in Marsham Street, SW1. The venue chosen was the West Pier, at Brighton, mainly because it had been the site of much location filming of Richard Attenborough's *Oh, What a Lovely War*, which was felt to be apposite to the business at hand. As a gesture, the team would provide transport between Brighton

Station and the West Pier and despite it being December, this was with a Southdown Titan PD3, sans roof and with doors locked in the open position. The lower saloon was occupied by a shivering Sir Berkeley and his immediate senior staff, while the junior minions were ordered to the upper-deck; where it was raining. Heavily

Having checked his notes, Sir Berkeley cleared his throat. 'At our last meeting, Mr Wood had a deferred question.' The Secretary turned to the United Counties GM. 'Which...was...?'

'Tring.'

'Tring?' Sir Berkeley summoned a file-holding minion. 'How long is a piece of Tring?' The minions giggled; the GMs were stoically po-faced.

'With respect Sir Berkeley, United Counties doesn't need it. We have a garage already, in nearby Aylesbury.'

Sir Berkeley appeared perplexed. 'Then what am I supposed to do with it?'

'Eh, stick it up your...' Simultaneously pulling Gerald Duckworth back into his seat and standing, Arthur White gestured to the COMS representative.

'Sir Berkeley, City of Oxford runs into Aylesbury with a number of routes., and to save on dead mileage, Tring would be a useful outpost.'

Tring went to COMS.

Once more, Sir Berkeley cleared his throat. 'Right, gentlemen, the Minister...'

'Wood Green.'

The Secretary gritted his teeth. 'What about it?'

It was Mr Bushrod, of Eastern National. 'Where does it go?'

'Go? Where is it? Should I have brought with me a map of southern England?'

'No, Sir Berkeley, just an A-Z.'

The ex-City Coach Co Wood Green garage remained with Eastern National.

Polishing his glasses, Sir Berkeley addressed the GMs. 'Gentleman, the Minister has determined that this will be our final meeting at which will be made irrevocable decisions concerning the issues confronting us, thus I and my delegation are all booked on this evening's 18.25 departure of the Brighton Belle. Now, I take it we are all agreed on vehicle policy, garage transfers, in finality, yes?'

The brouhaha was louder than that heard at the Pier's end when a winner of the Bingo jackpot was declared.

Arthur White was the first to stand. 'Sir Berkeley, since our last meeting, my fellow managers and I have discussed at length your proposals, to which we have all arrived at but one conclusion.'

Sir Berkeley grinned. 'Which is?'

'Ridiculous!'

'Mr White!'

'Sir Berkeley, how many bus companies have you managed, y'know, actually been at the sharp end, the front line? Ding, ding...'

The Secretary remained silent.

Glancing at his peers, Arthur White eye-balled the besieged knight. 'The largest block of buses you have on offer are the RT-type, totalling some 484 units or 67 percent of the Country Area fleet. The *newest* of these buses dates from 1954, some 14 to 15 years ago; the oldest are over 20 years old. Of modern rear-engined double-deckers, the best you can offer are three Leyland Atlanteans and eight Daimler Fleetlines. Mr Secretary, my Maidstone & District company owns the best part of some 200 rear-engined double-deckers, none of which is older than...*eight* years.' White gestured to the Ministry minions. 'I suggest one of these gents notes both carefully, and meticulously, what I am about to say.'

Arthur White looked at his audience of peers, all of whom were grinning from ear-to-ear. Winking at them, he turned to the Ministry minions. 'Sitting comfortably? Then I'll begin...'

His attention turned to the Secretary. 'Sir Berkeley, possibly suitable for our Medway Towns operations is the RML-type, the front-engined open rear-platform dinosaur. Therefore

M&D is prepared to take 50 of these museum pieces. However, the destination screen layout must be adapted to M&D standard, and the livery also, none of which modifications will be charged to my company, which doesn't require any more of the vehicles on offer.' White checked his notes. 'Whoops, nearly forgot. My company is prepared to pay £400 for each RML, or £18,000 for the whole 50. Not a penny more.'

As Chalky resumed his seat, Gerald Duckworth stood, before Sir Berkeley even had a chance to wipe his brow.

'Sir Berkeley, Southdown has an interest in a number of types you're offering, but with caveats. These are...'

Before the Southdown GM could continue, a Ministry minion took the microphone. 'Mr Duckworth, the operational characteristics of your company are well known. Therefore, it is mandated, or shall we say... *suggested* that Southdown takes the 69 RMC and 43 RCL types. After all, like all of your older double-deckers, these have enclosed platforms, with doors. Perfect, yes?'

Gerald Duckworth collapsed in a fit of giggles. Gathering his composure, he addressed the Ministry minion. 'Sir, with great respect, I know we're on a pleasure pier, but I thought the burlesque show didn't start here until...until, eh, seven-thirty?'

While Duckworth and his peers giggled, the minion remained unmoved, until a semblance of order was regained. Again, he stared at Duckworth. 'Meaning?'

Blowing his nose loudly, the Southdown GM attempted seriousness. 'Meaning? Meaning all 112 vehicles you mention are of AEC manufacture, and of which only one has a Leyland engine...'

'But Southdown has had AECs in the past?'

'Two. A double-decker demonstrator which never entered Southdown stock, and a Regal acquired and sold on immediately. Hardly a hotbed of AECs. However, if it is mandated that Southdown takes these vehicles, here's what you do. London Transport has some 300 Routemasters fitted with Leyland O.600 engines. You transfer some of those units into these AEC-powered RMC and RCL buses you're wishing on my company, at the same time convert them from epicyclic to synchromesh transmission, modify the destination screens accordingly and paint all of them into Southdown livery. And naturally, *not* at the expense of my company. Oh, and we'll take XF1-8, the Daimler Fleetlines. Again, all modifications and livery change at your expense.'

The minion checked *his* notes. 'What about the three Leyland Atlanteans?'

'Sir, Southdown doesn't operate any...'

As, amongst much chortling, Duckworth resumed his seat, another gent stood. 'Scully, Aldershot & District. Despite its antediluvian specification, I've always had a liking for the RF. Aldershot and District is prepared to accept 30 of these buses, subject to...' He looked around his peers. 'Transmission converted, together with the AEC AH470 engine substituted for the current A219 unit. Oh, and of course, re-liveried, and destination screens modified.'

The minion heaved a huge sigh. 'Pointless to ask who pays?'

In unison, from the gathered erupted a huge roar. 'Point...less!'

But Mr Scully wasn't finished. 'Given the extra duties we'll assume, my Aldershot company will transfer to Safeguard our routes within Guildford and district, for which work Safeguard will require a couple of double-deckers, which they've asked us to supply. These are

two Bristol Lodekkas, which will require re-engining, repainting and, modified screens. It goes without saying who will be responsible for the final payment of the foregoing and, if nobody's paying attention, it's neither A&D nor Safeguard!' To cheers and clapping, he resumed his seat. And immediately was up again. 'After all required modifications, my company is prepared to pay three-hundred pounds and fifteen shillings for each bus.'

It was then that stepped forward a visibly distraught Sir Berkeley. 'Gentlemen, perhaps this might be an opportune moment to recess for a repast?' He turned to the Trainee Davies. 'Young sir, where might be found the executive dining-room?'

'Well, there's the cafeteria. At the end of the pier...'

'Where are eating... ' Sir Berkeley gestured to the GMs. '...these people?'

Gerald Duckworth stepped forward. 'Luckily, through personal local contact, I've managed to obtain reservations at English's Fish and Oyster Bar, but unfortunately, the premises are somewhat small and thus I'm afraid they have room for only...thirteen.'

'Fine. Twelve of you chaps, and one of me.'

'Sir Berkeley, we're *thirteen*. You forgot Mr Davies, an intrinsic and important part of our team. Added to which, I'm given to understand the Pier offers a handsome fish 'n chips, *avec un Tizer premier cru...*'

The teams gathered together their papers.

'I'll take six!'

The full gathering froze. And then stared at the speaker. It was the GM of Luton Corporation. Arthur White was the first to respond.

'Six? Six of what?'

Mr R M C Baschy smiled. 'Six RTs'.

United Counties' J F Wood was outraged. 'Baschy, what the hell d'you think you're doing man? Have you

forgotten?'

Baschy shook his head. 'No, I haven't forgotten. But until then, I'm my own man, Luton buses is still my responsibility and we've just been thrown a lot more work. For which *I'll* need a few more buses. Cheap'. He turned to Sir Berkeley. 'Just paint them in our very basic livery, no other alterations, make sure they're the last to have gone through Aldenham and eighteen-hundred for the six. You pay for delivery. After all, it's only up the M1 or the A6, yeah?'

Gerald Duckworth patted on a shoulder of Sir Berkeley. 'There, Sir B.' Duckworth counted on his fingers. 'That only leaves with you another what...478, to sell?'

All adjourned for lunch. As Sir Berkeley walked dejectedly, his name was being paged. By a uniformed lady employee of the Pier.

'Burkeley, is there a Mr Burkeley here?'

'I'm *Sir* Berkeley.'

'Call for you, guv, in my office. Some lady by the name of Castle?'

Sir Berkeley scooted after her.

'Hello?'

'Sir Burkeley, how are things going down there? Remember, this all must be wrapped-up today, right, *today*?'

'Eh, yes Minister, today.'

'Well?'

'Eh, to use a cricket analogy, they've retired to the pavilion.'

The tone changed to one of more amiability. 'Of course, I'd forgotten, you're an accomplished cricketer...'

Sir Berkeley's chest puffed-out. 'Berkshire Colts second eleven, captain of Buckinghamshire first eleven...'

'Then might we be on the winning side?'

'Eh, bit of a sticky wicket.'

'Sticky? In what way?'

'Eh, price. What they're prepared to pay.'

'Is Daly down there with you?'

'Yes, Minister.'.

'Have him bowl when you think the over is ripe.'

'Our googly?'

'Our googly. And, Sir Burkeley, win. I don't want this to be a game of no-balls, understand?'

'Perfectly, Minister.' Sir Berkley stepped-out of the office, to be confronted by his team. 'Where you chaps off to?'

'Back to work. The cafeteria was closed...'

In direct contrast to the hungry men from the Ministry, jovial was the mood of the well-fed and well-wined delegation representing the provincial operating companies.

Sir Berkeley checked his watch. 'You're late.'

'Late? For what?' asked Arthur White. 'I don't recall a time-limit being placed on lunch.'

Sir Berkeley heaved the sigh of sighs. 'Mr White...do

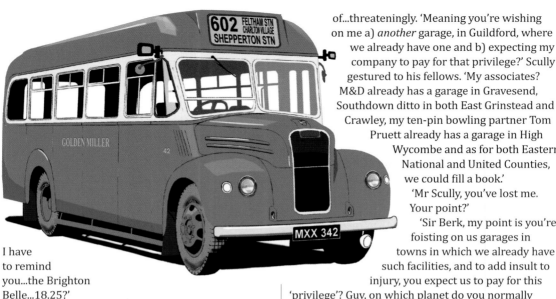

of...threateningly. 'Meaning you're wishing on me a) *another* garage, in Guildford, where we already have one and b) expecting my company to pay for that privilege?' Scully gestured to his fellows. 'My associates? M&D already has a garage in Gravesend, Southdown ditto in both East Grinstead and Crawley, my ten-pin bowling partner Tom Pruett already has a garage in High Wycombe and as for both Eastern National and United Counties, we could fill a book.'

'Mr Scully, you've lost me. Your point?'

'Sir Berk, my point is you're foisting on us garages in towns in which we already have such facilities, and to add insult to injury, you expect us to pay for this 'privilege'? Guv, on which planet do you normally reside?'

To roars of approval and cheers, Scully resumed his seat.

Seeing Sir Berkeley slump into his chair, Arthur White grabbed the moment. 'Sir Berkeley, knowing how important it is to make The Brighton Belle, tell you what...' He turned to the minions. 'Pencils sharpened and at the ready? Make sure you take this down, word for b----y word!'

To Sir Berkeley was being administered some *water*. He whispered in the ear of a minion. 'The second team, the asset, he's here?'

'Yes, Sir Berkeley...waiting.'

'Have him ready...now. Tell him the moment is his to choose. Make sure he understands.'

White surveyed the Ministry minions. 'Pay attention, like never before. Now, of the 17 lowbridge RLH buses, Thames Valley is prepared to accept these but only on condition they're re-engined with Gardner 5LW units, converted to manual transmission and painted into livery. City of Oxford will take the fourteen RC-type AEC Reliance and...'

'Hold on, hold it!' Emerging from the Ministry minions ranks was a person, unseen hitherto. He walked to the centre of the room.

'Daley, Arthur. Acting on and behalf of London Transport.' He scanned the opposing attendees. 'I'm sure you're all aware of the transfer of LT to the GLC? And as a result, there are a number of *our* routes which cross boundaries various and for which no operating subsidy will be forthcoming from the relevant counties.'

I have to remind you...the Brighton Belle...18.25?'

Gerald Duckworth spread his arms. 'Southdown Motor Services runs a very efficient hourly coach service from Brighton. Only six shillings and thruppence single, a journey of but two-and-a-half hours and given the number of your acolytes, we'd be happy to negotiate a party rate.'

Sir Berkeley was not amused. 'We need to finalize the vehicles question, and then will be addressed and resolved the other outstanding charges.'

Arthur White spun in his seat and looked at the other GMs. All were equally puzzled. Slowly, he turned to face Sir Berkeley. 'Other...charges? What...other charges?'

Sir Berkeley took another sip of the you-know-what. And it wasn't Tizer premier cru. 'Well, in addition to the cost of the vehicles, there is the question of freeholds.'

'Freeholds?' shouted Arthur White. 'What b----y freeholds?'

Sir Berkeley scratched his brow. 'Mr White, gentlemen. Being transferred to each of your companies is a total of 28 garages and surprise, surprise, London Transport is *not* a philanthropic body and thus expects to be recompensed for the freeholds of these properties at current market prices. Property values increase. It is your companies that will reap the benefit of a property boom.'

A gent stood. 'Scully, Aldershot & District. Eh... Duplication?'

'Duplication?' Sir Berkeley's brow furrowed. 'Meaning?'

To emphasize his point, Scully leant forward, sort

White, Duckworth, et al, all looked at each other, bemused.

Daley continued. 'Therefore, we, the LT, we don't want them, neither'. His visage broke into a Machiavellian-like smile. 'So we're giving them to... you!' He turned to another minion. 'Hand them out.' The minion was armed with maps of the then London Transport Central Area cross-boundary routes, a copy of which was given to each delegate.

'Now, as you are with map and can read, I don't propose to go into detail, just the routes, okay?'

Which is when flatulence overcame the somnolent and recumbent Sir Berkeley. Daley smiled. 'Obviously I have a seconder?'

Spin Doctor Daley took no prisoners. 'Okay, this is it. Aldershot & District will take over what were LT routes 71, 93, 164, 164A, 215, 219 and 237. Oh, and the 131. But only that section beyond Hampton Court Station, on which minimum fares will be charged as we'll continue running to West Molesey.' He eyed Scully. 'You'll need to renumber your bit, eh?' He scanned his notes. 'Right. Eastern National. You'll assume the 20 and 175, but only north of Romford, you understand? But you'll get the 205 and 205A, 242, 247, 250 and 287.' He looked around. As he had hoped, the delegation was overcome. 'Now, we at 55 Broadway are anxious to encourage into the former LPTA area newcomers, so Golden Miller...'

'A great horse!' Sir Berkeley was awakened pronto. 'Give me thirty-three to one against!'

Daley shook his head. 'Give him another glass of... of *water*.' The spinmeister continued. 'As I was saying, we'll pass to Golden Miller routes 203, 206 and 264.'

The delegates were stunned. A few struggled, writing notes copiously, and furiously.

Daley licked the lead of his pencil. 'Now...ah, yes! Maidstone & District. You get the 96, but no dropping-off /picking-up rights between

Woolwich and Bexleyheath unless the passenger is travelling to, or beyond the latter point. M&D will also operate the 99. Oh, yeah, also the 21A and of course, the 146.' Daley re-checked his notes. 'Hello...nearly missed it.' He looked-up. 'Golden Miller gets the 152. But only from Tolworth Broadway westwards.' He gestured to the Thames Valley GM. 'Mr Pruett, your company will assume routes 81, 81C, 90, 116, 117, 216, 218, 224 and 225. Some Heathrow workings there, nice little earners, eh?'

'Possibly...'.

Daley addressed the full assembly. 'You'll find us both approachable, amenable and... accommodating.'

Daley gestured to the snoring Sir Berkeley. 'Tell 'im we're on the homestretch, which means United Counties will take over the 84, 142, 158, the 292 and 292A, and the 298. Take it or leave it.' Daley gestured to Roger Davies. 'Think we, me, have forgotten anything?'

Davies was more than overcome by the direct question. He looked at his peers. 'I...I can say what troubles me?'

Arthur White smiled. 'You have the *conch*'.

'Pay differentials?'

The GMs looked at each other, as Davies warmed to his subject. 'Gents, Green Line crews are on higher rates than Country Bus crews. Who are on a higher scale than the crews employed by *your* companies. And those Central cross-boundary routes? How will these anomalies be addressed, and more importantly, who will pay to level them out?'

EPILOGUE

Which is when the lights flickered, and died.

Followed immediately by a voice from the darkness. 'Leave, nah! This 'all was only booked till five and it's nah gone six, well past the time you lot shoulda bin outta 'ere. Nah, scarper!'

The mysterious voice rang a handbell. Repeatedly. Which he kept ringing, and ringing and...ringing.

From the bedclothes appeared a hand, To press a button on the alarm, which stopped ringing. Drew shook his head sleepily, as appeared that of Dryhurst.

Drew eyed Dryhurst. 'I had this extraordinary dream...surreal.'

Dryhurst rubbed his eyes. 'I thought we were going to Showbus?'

Drew drew-apart the curtains. 'It's raining.'

Whereupon both turned over and returned to the Land of Nod...

Market Day
MEMORIES

BANBURY - The weekday market in the Oxfordshire town of Banbury is held on Thursdays. A Plaxton-bodied Volvo B10M of Pulham's Travel is pictured in September 2004 arriving on the service from Bourton-on-the-Water and Stow-on-the-Wold in neighbouring Gloucestershire. With the redevelopment of the town centre in recent years visiting coaches now drop passengers off in the bus station before parking elsewhere.

F or many centuries markets have been the focal point of communities for trading local produce and livestock. On certain days – usually a weekday and a Saturday – sellers and buyers would flock in from the surrounding areas and transform the market square and neighbouring streets into bustling hives of activity. During Victorian times many large and grand covered market halls were built up and down the country to accommodate traders and attract new growth.

In the early 1900s motorised people carriers, initially often converted lorries, brought people into the towns in larger numbers. A network of market-day bus services became established, provided in the main by small independent operators.

Market day buses used to be an important component of the rural bus network. **Mark Bailey** illustrates a selection.

In recent years the steady rise in car ownership has resulted in many of the services becoming unviable and consequently being withdrawn. Despite current shopping trends the popularity of local markets remains, but the impact on a town from the volume of visiting buses and coaches is a pale shadow of what it used to be.

This selection of photographs taken over the last 35 years depicts the scene in some of the busiest market towns in England and Wales.

RIGHT: **BOSTON - The Lincolnshire town of Boston holds its weekday market on a Wednesday. Seen departing the bus station in May 1985 is a Plaxton-bodied Ford R1114 belonging to Carnell's of Long Sutton. It is working the service across the Fens to Wisbech in Cambridgeshire.**

LEFT: **BURY ST EDMUNDS - Angel Hill in Bury St Edmunds used to be transformed on Wednesdays by an influx of coaches from rural Suffolk and beyond. Pictured in April 1983 about to return to Bacton with a full load is a Duple Dominant-bodied Bedford YRT of Mulley's Motorways. Nowadays market day services use the bus station rather than the town centre streets.**

RIGHT: **CARMARTHEN - The traditional weekday market in the south west Wales town of Carmarthen is on a Wednesday. Seen in June 1979 is a Duple Dominant-bodied Bedford YRQ from Lewis Coaches of Whitland, which has worked in on the service via Red Roses and St Clears. Loading behind is an ex-East Midland Duple-bodied Bedford VAM14 of Pioneer on the service to Laugharne and Pendine.**

DORCHESTER - Dorchester market on a Wednesday attracted a large number of vehicles, and the Trinity Street bus park in the town centre was the focal point. For almost 60 years Bere Regis & District sustained a large network of routes throughout rural Dorset, many of which only ran on market days. Pictured in May 1984 on the Little Bredy service is a rare Plaxton-bodied Leyland Panther, new to Seamarks of Luton.

HITCHIN - The Hertfordshire town of Hitchin holds its weekday market on a Tuesday. In later years Premier Travel of Cambridge was probably better known for its coach services to Luton, Heathrow and Gatwick airports, but the company also operated a handful of local routes. Pictured in April 1990 is a Plaxton-bodied AEC Reliance working the Tuesdays-only service from Royston.

LAUNCESTON - Tuesday is market day in the Cornish town of Launceston. Pictured in July 1987 is a Plaxton-bodied Bedford YMT of Fry's, which has worked in from its home village of Tintagel on the north Cornwall coast via Boscastle and Camelford. Fry's distinctive yellow and blue coaches with the knight on horseback insignia are sadly now just a memory.

LOUTH - Louth in Lincolnshire holds weekday markets on Wednesdays and Fridays. When this photograph was taken in May 1985, Applebys was the largest independent in Lincolnshire, with a network of services spanning much of the county. Seen on a Wednesday parked in the bus station, the Plaxton-bodied Leyland Tiger on the left has worked in from Market Rasen, and the Plaxton-bodied Bedford YMT on the right has brought shoppers in from Caistor and Binbrook.

NEWTON ABBOT - The midweek market in the South Devon town of Newton Abbot is on a Wednesday. Pictured laying over in November 1984 is an ex-London Country ECW-bodied Bristol LHS6L of Wood Brothers, which was working the service from the Dartmoor village of Widecombe-in-the-Moor and Buckfastleigh.

SALISBURY - The New Canal terminus in Salisbury city centre is still used today for the few Tuesday and Saturday market day services that remain, but is nowhere near as busy as this scene from a Tuesday in July 1985. Pictured with a full load returning to the Wiltshire village of Sutton Veny is an ex-Eastern Scottish Alexander-bodied Bedford YRT of Beeline of Warminster. Parked behind is a pair of Duple Dominant-bodied Bedfords, one from Herringtons of Fordingbridge on the service to Whitsbury in Hampshire, and one from Nadder Valley of Tisbury on the service to Ridge.

YEOVIL - Tuesdays and Fridays are market days in the Somerset town of Yeovil. Pictured laying over in the bus station on a Friday in August 1981 is a rare ECW-bodied AEC Swift of Brutonian, which had been new to Lowestoft Corporation (where ECW was based), having worked in from its home town of Bruton. Just visible alongside is a Duple-bodied Bedford SB3 of Pearce, Darch & Willcox (Comfy Lux) on the service from Dorchester.

TRURO- The city of Truro is the administrative centre of Cornwall, and holds a market each Wednesday. This picture, taken in February 1988 in the bus station at Lemon Quay, shows a pair of coaches from the fleet of Williams of St Agnes. The Plaxton-bodied Bedford YNT on the left is waiting to return on the market day service to Trevellas, and the Duple Dominant-bodied Bedford YMT on the right is working the regular weekday service to St Agnes on the north Cornwall coast.

This Scania OmniCity was new to Menzies Aviation at Heathrow Airport in 2003. It is squeezing through the smaller of two archways on the Castle Howard estate whilst working between Malton and York.

Stephensons
OF Easingwold

David Longbottom shows some of the varied vehicles operated by one of North Yorkshire's biggest independent operators.

Stephensons of Easingwold is a family-owned bus and coach operator based at two locations in North Yorkshire, at Tholthorpe and Kirkbymoorside. It began operations around 1990 and now has a fleet of some 80 vehicles of all sizes.

Around 50 North Yorkshire County Council school contracts are operated together with a range of bus services, mainly in the Hambleton and Ryedale districts. The fleet varies from 16-seat minibuses through to double-deckers. About half the fleet is made up of full-size coaches with Volvo being the preferred make, although other manufacturers are featured.

The fleet numbering system is of interest, many vehicles carrying a four-digit number of which the first two digits denote the seating capacity, although this has fallen out of use over the last couple of years.

An ADL Enviro200, purchased new in 2013, passes through Helperby on a short working of service 29 from Easingwold to Shipton-by-Beningbrough.

A 60-seat Enviro300 waits during a torrential downpour at Shipton-by-Beningbrough for a connecting bus from York before doing a short working to Tholthorpe. The bus was new in 2005 to Courtney Coaches of Bracknell.

Seen in Easingwold's Market Place is an East Lancs-bodied Scania N113 which had been new in 1994 to Midland Fox as M163 GRY, but has been re-registered VEZ 9645. It was bought by Stephensons in 2009 from Arriva Midlands North.

Another ex-Arriva bus, this time from Kent & Sussex, is this 1998 Mercedes-Benz Vario with Plaxton Beaver 2 body. It is arriving in Barton-le-Street while working from Malton to Hovingham.

A 1996 Plaxton Beaver-bodied Mercedes-Benz 709D is seen going over New Bridge level crossing on the North Yorkshire Moors Railway on the Pickering to Rosedale Abbey service.

This Alexander RL-bodied Leyland Olympian was new to Stagecoach's United Counties business in 1990, and for most of its days was a Huntingdon bus, staying in the town during the Premier Buses and Huntingdon & District operations, passing back to Stagecoach in the Fens in 2008, before heading north to Stephensons in 2009. It is seen near the village of Nawton in the Ryedale countryside.

Personalised registration J9 SOE is carried by this Wright Endurance-bodied Volvo B10B, one of three acquired from Arriva the Shires in 2009; the three were new to Sovereign in 1995. This bus was previously M103 UKX, and is seen on the cobbles of Easingwold Market Place having just arrived with the direct service from York via the A19.

The majority of Stephensons coaches are Volvos, but other marques do feature such as this Ikarus-bodied DAF, like a number in the fleet now upseated to 70 – as indicated by the 7008 fleet number - to replace a double-decker on a school contract. This coach was unusual in being new to the US Army in the UK in 2001, joining Stephensons in 2010 from Weavers of Newbury. It is in Knaresborough between workings on contract 657H to the Pateley Bridge area.

A more typical coach is this Volvo, a 12.8m-long B9M with Plaxton Panther body, delivered in 2013. It is seen at Hull's KC Stadium. It is an air-conditioned 53-seater with centre toilet alongside the continental door.

New to Blue Bus of Horwich in 2002 was Ikarus Polaris-bodied DAF SB220 seen at Helmsley Market Place awaiting departure for York. This bus was sold in 2013.

Battle of Trafalgar

A small batch of ex-Midland Red D9s, built by the company in-house, were among the more unlikely open-toppers to be seen on the Round London Sightseeing Tour in 1983.

When it comes to taking bus photographs, London's Trafalgar Square has always offered rich pickings, says **Peter Rowlands** – providing you're prepared to take your chance among the throning tourists who frequent it in all seasons

All photographs by the author.

Whether you live in London or have only visited the city once, you must surely have found yourself drawn irresistibly to Trafalgar Square. It might seem rather an obvious place to go (more than 15 million visitors a year would probably agree), but that's just a testament to its magnetic quality.

In the bus world it has particular significance. Not only is it served by around 20 London routes (not to mention innumerable sightseeing buses and tourist coaches); it also offers unbeatable open views in every direction. Even in the dead of winter, when tall buildings cast shadows across surrounding streets, you can usually rely on photographing buses there

in unobscured sunshine (assuming there's any to be had).

Architecturally, the imposing Victorian buildings provide a dramatic backdrop: William Wilkins' National Gallery façade, James Gibbs' St-Martins-in-the-Fields, Robert Smirke's Canada House – all from the early part of the nineteenth century – and South Africa House and Admiralty Arch from the early twentieth.

And of course in the centre, William Railton's Nelson's Column and Edward Lutyens' fountains, along with Edwin Landseer's lions.

Until 2003 the square formed the centrepiece of a one-way traffic system (effectively it was a large roundabout), but then the north side (the street in

Emerging from Northumberland Avenue in October 1985 is a former London Transport DM class Daimler Fleetline with Ensignbus, running under Culturebus branding, which Ensignbus acquired from former operator Trathens.

A number of RCL Routemaster coaches acquired from London Country Bus Services by London Transport, with doors removed, were allocated to round-London tour work. This one is seen in 1986.

Grey-Green ran these colourful Alexander-bodied Volvo Citybuses on the first tendered route in the central area to be awarded to an independent, This one, seen soon after entering service in November 1988, was later repainted into Arriva's "bull-horn" red livery, still on route 24.

Before 2003, buses ran along the north side of Trafalgar Square. Seen here turning at the north-east corner in 1989 is a Leyland Titan on the 22B – the eastern half of then-recently divided route 22 to Homerton. The route was cut back to Tottenham Court Road later, then discontinued altogether in 1998.

Seen in May 1989, this ECW coach-bodied Leyland Olympian was run on a Reading-London commuter service by Bee Line (formerly Alder Valley North).

New to Scottish operator Parks of Hamilton, this Caetano-bodied Volvo B10M had found its way into the Eastbourne Borough Transport fleet by the time it was photographed in August 1990.

front of the National Gallery) was pedestrianised, and all east-west traffic was routed along the south side, where a much smaller roundabout was created at the top of Whitehall.

This now provides a beguiling platform for photographing buses travelling in almost every direction – though you have to pick your moment to avoid tourists, and if you're not standing far enough back you'll need a rather wide-angle setting.

The pedestrianisation had the odd effect of reversing the traffic flow on the road running along the west side of the square. For many years, buses on route 15 would lurk here, facing north, before continuing round the square to start their return journey eastwards. Now the flow is southbound, and the lurking has ceased.

Six main roads feed into Trafalgar Square, though two of them have no scheduled bus services. One of the latter is the Mall, which is closed to all commercial traffic, and the other is Northumberland Avenue, a broad but relatively short street connecting the square to the Embankment. However, some turning buses do use Northumberland Avenue – notably Transport for London's heritage Routemasters – and it's also used by sightseeing buses.

The other four roads serving the square are Cockspur Street (leading west into Pall Mall, and used by many routes to and from Piccadilly Circus); the Strand (running east); Whitehall (running south); and St Martin's Place (leading north into Charing Cross Road).

Many of London's longest-serving and most famous bus routes pass the square, including the 9 (Aldwych to Hammersmith), the 11 (Liverpool Street to Fulham), the 12 (Oxford Circus to Dulwich), and the 15 (Trafalgar Square to Blackwall). Until the final cull of Routemasters in the early 2000s, nearly a dozen routes through the square were served by these stalwarts.

As I write this, Routemasters on two heritage routes (the 9 and the 15) still terminate here, though those on the 9 were withdrawn in the summer of 2014.

Perhaps because of its proximity to the corridors of power, Trafalgar Square has tended to be one of the first places to see innovative London buses or liveries. No doubt their operators or instigators were keen to have their work paraded on routes where politicians were particularly likely to see them.

A classic instance of this phenomenon came in 1988, when route 24 (which also runs past the

This notably half-hearted all-over red livery was used by MTL London, the Merseyside Transport offshoot, in the later days of its operations in the capital. It is seen in 1997, a year before withdrawal.

Houses of Parliament) was the first in central London to be put out to competitive tender. Grey-Green (a forerunner of Arriva) operated the service with Alexander-bodied Volvo double-deckers in a suitable livery of grey and green with orange lining: difficult to miss amid a sea of red.

No doubt a similar impulse prompted Mayor Boris Johnson's office to push for the first production New Routemasters to be put on route 24 in June 2013. Meanwhile, back in 2003, route 453 from Marylebone to Deptford was one of the first in central London to use artics. The Mercedes-Benz Citaros remained on the route for eight years.

Over the years, Trafalgar Square has been on the schedule of a variety of services from out of town. It used to be visited by London Transport's Green Line coaches (notably on route 709), and in the late 1980s you could see two competing commuter services between London and Reading, run by Reading Transport and Bee Line respectively. Both used Leyland Olympian double-deckers, though with its ECW coach bodywork and yellow livery, Bee Line's contribution was arguably the more arresting.

There is still a 701 Green Line service from Reading to London, now run by First with Wright-bodied double-deckers, but it terminates at Victoria coach station.

While the traffic flow remodelling of 2003 may have been designed to improve the lot of pedestrians,

An exuberant vertical yellow ribbon motif was London Central's idea of route branding for the number 12. This RML was photographed in August 1995.

Mercedes-Benz Citaro artics operated by Stagecoach ran on the 453 for eight years.

Operated by Citybus during its brief foray into central London tendering, this Alexander-bodied Volvo Olympian is seen emerging from the Strand in July 1997, when the road layout made it easier than it is now to take pictures from this angle.

There were 24 DAF DB250s with Optare Spectra bodywork operated by London Central on route 3 from 1992 to 2000. This picture dates from September 1998.

This three-axle MCW Metrobus, seen in 2006 running for The Big Bus Company, was formerly with China Motor Bus, Hong Kong, and features full-height Alexander-style upper-deck front windows, which Metrobuses built for the UK never had.

An Alexander Dennis Enviro400 of Metroline heading south from Trafalgar square in September 2012, with a similar bus of London General to the right.

An Alexander Dennis Enviro400 of London General on route 24 in May 2008.

An unusual Caetano Optimo-bodied Toyota of Clarkes of London, seen in 2009.

Among more unusual recent open-toppers bought new by Big Bus Tours is a batch of three-axle models built in China by Anhui Ankai Automobile. This one heads down Whitehall in 2012.

it's debatable whether it did much for road traffic. In busy times the traffic entering the square from the east often backs up far down the Strand; and from the west, even in quiet periods, it can take an age for buses to advance even a few vehicle lengths along the single-lane access from Haymarket into Cockspur Street. This leaves plenty of time for photographers to plan their shots, but it's pretty tedious if you happen to be on the bus.

In the 35 years that I've been photographing London buses, Trafalgar Square has proved an ideal location to chronicle the gradual change in London buses: the survival, then decline of the Routemasters; the emergence of privatised London bus companies; route tendering, with its colourful new liveries; some wacky examples of route branding; the emergence of differentiated red liveries and fleetnames; then their disappearance with the spread of all-over red.

And latterly, there's been the gradual proliferation of New Routemasters, which were already running on three routes past the square when I wrote this article (the 9, the 11 and the 24), and are likely to appear on more.

Instead of the former square-cut and big-windowed

A New Routemaster on the 24 in February 2014, followed by an old Routemaster on heritage route 15.

double-deckers, we are seeing a more rounded, almost hooded look.

That's not the end of the story, of course. Nothing stays the same for long. The traffic flows may change again; other buses will eventually appear. One thing is for sure – if you want to be part of the passing scene, and to chart it in all its majesty, Trafalgar Square has to be high on your priority list.

Edinburgh demonstrators

The main bus operator in Edinburgh has a long tradition of borrowing buses from other companies and trialling new designs or types of vehicles. **Richard Walter** illustrates some of the vehicles tested by Lothian Region Transport and Lothian Buses over the past 25 years.

LRT borrowed Leyland Lynx G747 PNN from Nottingham City Transport in 1990 and ran it on service 80 to Polton Mill in Midlothian. An order was placed for 12 Lynxes which were delivered in 1991.

The Alexander bodywork on 1990 Scania demonstrator G879 TVS was similar to that fitted to LRT's own fleet of Olympians. Billed as "The Cleaner Quieter Bus", it was trialled on service 23 between Morningside and Trinity. The bus, pictured at the Morningside terminus, was later to operate with Strathclyde's Buses in all-over orange.

LEFT: **LRT was interested in the Dennis Dart some time before ordering its own examples. This short 1992 Dart with Plaxton Pointer body, London United DR112 (J112 DUV), is seen at Marchmont on service 24. It was also operated by Eastern Scottish.**

RIGHT: **Following the purchase of a batch of Leyland Lynxes, LRT considered a number of options for replacement of its Leyland Nationals. Safle-bodied Volvo B10L L456 JCK was painted in fleet colours during 1996. It ran as 156 – loosely matching the registration - and was mainly to be found on route 13 between Findlay Gardens and Blackhall. It is seen at Charlotte Square.**

LEFT: **LRT tried this 1992 40-seat Wright-bodied Dart demonstrator, LDZ 6040, on service 24. It is seen at the terminal point at St Andrew Square. This body style was known as the Handybus. When it ceased running as a Wright demonstrator it was sold to Yorkshire Traction and re-registered J416 CWF.**

DAF SB220 R29 GNW with Plaxton Prestige body was the first gas bus trialled in Edinburgh. It spent a short while in 1998 running on service 13 from Marine depot between Lochend and Findlay Gardens. It was later operated by Arriva and, converted to diesel, returned to Scotland running for Arriva Scotland West.

This Dennis Dart SLF with Caetano Nimbus body, V674 FPO, carried a running board rather than a full destination blind. It is at the Lochend terminus of service 13 in the summer of 2000.

LEFT: **The trial of a Mercedes-Benz Citaro, BU53 AYA, took place in 2003 on cross city service 22 from the Gyle Centre to Ocean Terminal. It is seen arriving at the Ocean Terminal terminus. It was the second Citaro to be tried, following an earlier 02-registered bus.**

RIGHT: **The first articulated bus appeared in 2005 when Hispano-bodied Volvo B7LA FJ53 LZX arrived, with harlequins and Lothian fleet names added to its London red livery. Because of its length, the vehicle could only be used from Marine depot with its large entrance ramp and appeared mainly on part workings of service 26. Although it did not carry a fleet number, the bus was referred to on its tickets as being 888. Here it is setting out from St Andrew Square to Clerwood along Princes Street, now a location for trams as well as buses. It was sold by Volvo to Manchester Airport.**

LEFT: **Seen heading through Cameron Toll in 2005 is Scania OmniDekka SN04 CPE which carried fleet number 999 and was painted in full harlequin livery. It ran on frequent services 37/37A between Silverknowes and Penicuik in Midlothian.**

RIGHT: **Continuing its evaluation of articulated buses, in 2008 Scania OmniCity YN54 ALO was allocated fleet number 50 and painted in the park-and-ride livery of service X48 which operated from sites at Ingliston and Sheriffhall. The articulated bus provided additional capacity at peak times.**

LEFT: **Lothian Buses re-examined the concept of gas-powered buses in 2012 when it ran Caetano-bodied MAN EcoCity demonstrator WX61 FLO on service 49 between The Jewell and Rosewell in Midlothian. It was one of the first examples of a Euro 6 compliant bus in Scotland.**

RIGHT: **DRZ 9713 was one of two Wrightbus StreetLites which have been evaluated by Lothian Buses. It ran on service 1 between Clermiston and Easter Road in 2013 and is seen in London Road. It is a DF – Door Forward – model with 44 seats.**

Lothian Buses runs 15 ADL Enviro400H hybrids, but during 2013 it tried SN61 DFK, a standard diesel Enviro400 alongside the hybrids on service 10 between Western Harbour and Torphin to compare performance.

The most recent demonstrator in the Lothian Buses fleet, in the spring of 2014, has been this Euro 6 Volvo B5TL with Wrightbus Gemini 3 body, BF63 HDC, which featured a glass panel to the offside on the staircase. It is seen leaving the Hunter's Tryst terminus of service 27 on route to Silverknowes, chosen for the evaluation because of the hilly sections on the route. After trying the bus an order was placed for 25.

The Bristol SC4LK had been introduced in 1956, designed as a lightweight bus primarily for rural service. It had a front-mounted Gardner 4LK engine, and an ECW body with a full-width cab. Production ended in 1961. The biggest concentration of SC models was to be found in the east of England, with Lincolnshire and Eastern Counties being significant users of the type which, with its 57bhp engine, was perhaps best suited to relatively flat terrain. This is a 1960 Lincolnshire bus in Scunthorpe in 1972.

A decade of change at Bristol

The 1960s was a decade of change for Bristol Commercial Vehicles. **Geoff Mills** illustrates the models produced by the company in that period.

ABOVE: **Most Bristol MW models had six-cylinder engines, but a minority were powered by the five-cylinder Gardner 5HLW, including this 45-seat bus in the fleet of United Automobile Services. It was new in 1960.**

BELOW: **The Lodekka was one of Bristol's most successful models. The original LD series was discontinued in 1961, with the last examples going to Scottish Bus Group companies. This is a 1960 LD6G with 60-seat ECW body in the fleet of Scottish Omnibuses in Edinburgh. In this 1976 view, near the end of its life, it is still smart.**

ABOVE: **This 1963 United MW has the more common Gardner 6HLW engine. The basic ECW body structure is the same as on the bus illustrated on the previous page, but it has 39 high-backed seats, hence the cream and red dual-purpose livery. Note also the use of cream rubber mountings for the side windows.**

BELOW: **The Bristol RE was the most successful of the rear-engined single-deck chassis launched in the UK in the 1960s. This is a 1964 RELH6G from the Lincolnshire fleet, photographed in Baldock in 1966. Its ECW body seated 47. The chrome wheel trims were a popular feature on 1960s coaches.**

ABOVE: **The original LD model Lodekka was replaced by the improved FS, as seen here with a 60-seat FS6G in the fleet of Alexander Fife. This bus was new in 1964. It was photographed outside the company's Kirkcaldy depot in 1976.**

BELOW: **Latterly Lodekka production was concentrated on the 30ft-long 70-seat FLF. This Thames Valley bus, an FLF6G, was new in 1965 and is seen looking a bit battered in Windsor two years later.**

The availability of Bristol chassis on the open market attracted a number of BET group companies, and at the end of the 1960s Aldershot & District ordered 15 RELL6Gs with dual-door 44-seat Marshall bodies. They were delivered in 1970. A&D had previously bought AECs for its single-deck fleet.

The underfloor-engined SU took over from the front-engined SC as Bristol's country bus model. This is the 28ft-long SUL4A version, with 36-seat ECW body, in the United fleet. The 4A part of the chassis code indicated the use of a four-cylinder Albion engine. Like the SC, the SU was 7ft 6in wide. It was built between 1960 and 1966.

Through a share exchange with British Leyland in 1965, sales of Bristol chassis and ECW bodies were no longer restricted to state-owned operators. A number of municipals placed orders with Bristol, including the Stalybridge, Hyde, Mossley and Dukinfield Joint Board which in 1967 took three RESL6Gs with 43-seat Northern Counties bodies.

A 1967 RELL6G with ECW's bus-style body but fitted with 50 high-backed seats for interurban operation. The operator was United Automobile. The open doors show the shallow three-step entrance.

The most successful of Bristol's light chassis was the LH, which was launched in 1967 and replaced the SU. It was offered in three lengths and this is the most common model, the LH with 45-seat ECW bus body. It is a 1969 bus in the fleet of United Counties. It was an LH6L with Leyland O.400 engine.

The successor to the Lodekka was the rear-engined VRT. An early user was Scottish Omnibuses, which took batches in 1968 and 1969. This is a 1969 bus with 77-seat ECW body, a useful 10% increase in capacity over a standard FLF Lodekka. The VRT was not a success in Scotland, and all of those delivered to the Scottish Bus Group were withdrawn in the early 1970s, most going to the National Bus Company in exchange for Lodekkas.

Perhaps the most impressive members of the RE range were the 12m-long REMH6Gs delivered to Western SMT and Scottish Omnibuses for services between Scotland and London. These had Alexander M-type bodies with 42 reclining seats, a toilet, oil-fired heating and double glazing – quite a specification for a 1960s coach. This is a 1969 Western SMT coach in London's Victoria Coach Station soon after entering service.

Among the more unusual Bristol LH models were compact Marshall-bodied buses delivered to NBC subsidiaries Western National and Southern Vectis. The latter received four in 1969. The short chassis was the LHS, and the Southern Vectis buses were 35-seater

LBA link

Tony Greaves illustrates a selection of the vehicles which have been used to link Leeds with Leeds Bradford Airport

All photographs by the author.

B us services, express or otherwise, to Leeds Bradford Airport were not conspicuous at the height of my camera-carrying walks around Leeds, with just the occasional sightings of West Yorkshire Road Car Bristol LS and MW coaches seeming to fulfil obligations.

They weren't the most suitable for the job, being underfloor-engined with little space for luggage inside, so that it had to go in the boot. It was very much a coach link as, after the Leeds pick-ups at Vicar Lane and Wellington Street, it ran non-stop to the airport. As if to make the point that the operation was begrudged, they had destinations wound to a blank and always had 'Airport' on a card in the windscreen.

A regular performer on airport duties was an ex-Tillings Transport Bristol LS which was acquired in 1965 and was withdrawn from service in 1973. The ECW-bodied Bristol RELH6G was next type seen on

West Yorkshire's former Tillings Transport Bristol LS in Wellington Street, Leeds, on its way from Wellington Street Coach Station to Vicar Lane Bus Station, both of which are long closed. There is an 'Airport' bill in the nearside windscreen.

airport duties, but by this time several of the batch had been rebuilt by Willowbrook with famously unfortunate results. At least they were proper dual-purpose vehicles with easy boarding and alighting, but they still had no provision for extra luggage. By this time the route was known as the X84 and ran to the airport from the West Yorkshire bus stations in Leeds.

In December 1982 my new wife and I moved into our Horsforth, near Leeds, home, situated under the flightpath for the main runway. Leeds Bradford Airport is the highest in England at an elevation of 681ft. We moved in at an interesting time, as planned improvements to the airport had started and were completed in November 1984. This included an extension to the main runway, which required the construction of twin tunnels to take the A658 Bradford to Harrogate road beneath the runway.

Displaying its comprehensive Airporter branding and an unusual door rebuild, a West Yorkshire Plaxton-bodied Leopard climbs New Road Side into Horsforth.

As if to highlight the point that the airport could now accept larger long-haul aircraft, the extension was officially opened on 4 November 1984 with the first jumbo jet to land there, a Canadian Wardair Boeing 747 which inaugurated regular flights to Toronto. A chartered British Airways 747 soon joined the entertainment watched by a huge crowd as these giants perform low passes.

Steady growth of the airport prompted a similar growth in bus services, mainly from Leeds, but also from Bradford and Harrogate

West Yorkshire Road Car had operated an express service from Leeds for some years, officially the X84, but often the only destination display was 'Leeds', still supplemented by a card with the word 'Airport' in the windscreen. That changed in the summer of 1986 when West Yorkshire, under contract to the PTE, launched a new dedicated express service,

the MetroBus Airporter with, at last, appropriate branding, including the airport logo on the vehicles and publicity. The buses were in fact relegated Leyland Leopard coaches that had been rebuilt by fitting two piece glider-type doors. These were actually bus doors and because they were flat they had to be contained by a boxy extension to the top of the doorway in the curved Plaxton bodywork. The service ran daily, every hour, except Sundays, from Leeds Central Bus Station.

In August 1986, an Air France Concorde charter flight from Paris landed at Leeds Bradford for the first time, and an estimated 60,000 people were there to see it. Occasional Concorde charter flights, all of which used British Airways aircraft, continued until June 2000, just one month before the Concorde disaster in Paris.

Yorkshire Rider took over operations of the West

One of the hitherto attractive ECW-bodied Bristol RELHs that were subjected to rebuilds by Willowbrook that, to say the least, compromised their appearance. A proper Leeds-Bradford Airport blind is displayed. It is outside West Yorkshire's Vicar Lane Bus Station which is now a car park.

Awaiting departure on the newly resurfaced bus stop at the airport is First's Dennis Dart SLF with Plaxton Pointer body, showing off its joint LBA/Metro branding.

Yorkshire PTE in October 1986 and in 1989 acquired the Leeds and Bradford operations of the West Yorkshire Road Car Company. In 1994 Yorkshire Rider was purchased by the Badgerline Group, which eventually became a constituent part of FirstBus. Deregulation of bus services in October 1986 saw a tendering system introduced for the airport services, so that the operator with the best (ie lowest) response to a tender usually won the job for the next period before re-tendering came round. This prompted coach companies, not always used to, or suited to bus operation, to tender for the work.

Coach operator Godson of Crossgates operated the 757 Leeds route on an hourly frequency using a pair of Ikarus-bodied DAFs, hired from what was then the Hughes DAF dealership. Prominent 'LBA Airlink' and 'Daily link to & from Bradford & Leeds City Centres' graphics were carried between the wheelbase along with those for the PTE and the airport on the rear overhang. Godson relinquished the contract early and the two buses that had worked between the two cities of Leeds and Bradford, linking them to the airport, were replaced by First in Leeds with a single Plaxton-bodied Dennis Dart.

A Guiseley coach company, Aztecbird, had as one of its directors the former Independent Coachways engineer, who at that company had been involved with airport transfer work. Possibly he was attracted to the high-profile nature

of the routes serving the airport, and Aztecbird became the next airport bus operator.

Its fleet included a pair of low-floor Neoplans, one of which was exhibited at the first Expocoach show at Castle Donnington in October 1990. It appeared under the dealer's banner, with little to say it was based on a Hungarian Csepel chassis, with Raba-MAN axles and a Cummins engine. This and its fellow are believed to be the only examples of this early low-floor bus built in right-hand-drive form and both found a home with Hallmark of Luton, later both migrating north to Aztecbird. As was to be expected from Neoplan, they had up-to-date styling and Aztecbird's Service 757 livery of white with blue, red and yellow presented a modern image. Despite their impressive appearance and the reliability of the engine and driveline, a vulnerable waterpipe under the rear overhang could let them down, leading to overheating and they were later joined in service by a pair of DAF/Ikarus Polaris buses hired from Hughes DAF. The 757 service was extended via Pool in Wharfedale, to Otley, some 25 minutes beyond Leeds Bradford Airport during Aztecbird's period of operation.

In February 2007 First started an express coach service from York, at £10 single and £15 return, but it never really took off and most coaches seemed to carry mostly fresh air. Not surprisingly, the

ABOVE: **An ex-Menzies Aviation Scania OmniCity departs Leeds City Station on the first day of Centrebus operation of the 757 in April 2010. It is in the previous owner's livery, with the addition of Airport Direct branding. On repaint in to Centrebus livery a silhouette of an aircraft was added to the branding.**

BELOW: **Approaching the site of the coach station on Wellington Street is one of the two DAF SB220s with Ikarus bodies operated by Godson's Coaches. LBA – which flanks the destination screen - is the IATA code for Leeds Bradford Airport**

The airport terminal provides a backdrop for one of the two Neoplan low-floor buses on Hungarian Csepel chassis operated by Aztecbird on the 757.

service was discontinued.

In April 2010, Centrebus started operation of three Leeds Bradford Airport bus services that amounted to a small network. Routes 737 from Bradford to Harrogate; 747 from Bradford to the Airport, and the 757 from Leeds all featured prominent 'Airport Direct' branding from the start. The initial fleet of fast and comfortable Scania OmniCity CN94UBs, all previously operated by Menzies Aviation at Heathrow, proved to be a useful buy, and they were the first to be used on a service to the airport to be specially equipped for such duties, with extensive luggage racking in the front portion of the saloon.

The company faced competition as First continued to run the 757 service between the airport and Leeds railway station, while Centrebus ran to Leeds Central Bus Station. Since July 2010 Centrebus has been the only operator of route 757 after First withdrew its service. Frequency has become more useful too, with a half-hourly daytime service, reducing to hourly during the evening. From time to time ordinary buses from Centrebus's Leeds garage operated airport duties, and anything from an ex-London Optare Olympus Scania to a new MCV Evolution on chassis by either Dennis, VDL, or for a short time before they were transferred away, MAN.

In September 2013 Arriva bought out its partners in Centrebus and rebranded the company Yorkshire

One of Aztecbird's pair of Ikarus Polaris bodied DAFs shows the distinctive 757 route branding.

Tiger. A new livery of all-over orange with black tiger stripes is gradually replacing that of Centrebus.

Another operator seen on airport services is Bradford-based TLC Travel, whose 967 links Menston, Otley and Leeds Bradford Airport, using Optare SlimLine Solos and ADL Enviro200s.

In terms of passenger throughput Leeds Bradford was the UK's 16th busiest airport in 2012 and Jet2.com, Monarch Airlines and Ryanair are based there. Thomson Airways have a seasonal base at the airport. The airport bus service network will continue to provide interest as the airport continues to grow.